Teacher Acculturation

# Teacher Acculturation

*Stories of Pathways to Teaching*

By

Edward R. Howe

BRILL

LEIDEN | BOSTON

Cover illustration: Photograph by Edward R. Howe

All chapters in this book have undergone peer review.

The Library of Congress Cataloging-in-Publication Data is available online at https://catalog.loc.gov

Typeface for the Latin, Greek, and Cyrillic scripts: "Brill". See and download: brill.com/brill-typeface.

ISBN 978-90-04-50357-1 (paperback)
ISBN 978-90-04-50358-8 (hardback)
ISBN 978-90-04-50359-5 (e-book)

Copyright 2022 by Koninklijke Brill NV, Leiden, The Netherlands.
Koninklijke Brill NV incorporates the imprints Brill, Brill Nijhoff, Brill Hotei, Brill Schöningh, Brill Fink, Brill mentis, Vandenhoeck & Ruprecht, Böhlau Verlag and V&R Unipress.
All rights reserved. No part of this publication may be reproduced, translated, stored in a retrieval system, or transmitted in any form or by any means, electronic, mechanical, photocopying, recording or otherwise, without prior written permission from the publisher. Requests for re-use and/or translations must be addressed to Koninklijke Brill NV via brill.com or copyright.com.

This book is printed on acid-free paper and produced in a sustainable manner.

*To my parents*

# Contents

**Foreword** XI
    *Ruth Hayhoe*
**Dedication** XIII
**List of Acronyms** XIV
**Guide to the Reader** XVI

**Prologue** 1
  1  Learning to Read: The Importance of Support from Home  4
  2  Learning to Write: The Significance of Teachers  5
  3  Learning to Research: Finding a Niche for a Life's Work  6
  4  Traditional Didactic Teaching: The Antithesis of My Teaching Philosophy  7
  5  Learning to Enjoy Writing Again: An Undergraduate Transformation  7
  6  Learning a Foreign Language in an Immersion Classroom  9
  7  Memory Box: Stories from a Teacher's Briefcase  10

**Introduction: Comparative Ethnographic Narrative**  12
  1  Teacher-to-Teacher Conversations  13
  2  Teacher Educator-to-Teacher Educator Conversations  14
  3  Evolution of a Teacher Educator's Conceptual Framework  15
  4  Summary  17

**1 Hazel: Chinese-Canadian Home Economics Teacher (1949–1984)**  19
  1  The Journey to Becoming a Teacher  19
  2  Reflections on Race and Ethnicity  22
  3  Reflections on Equity for Novice Teachers  24
  4  Reflections on Being a Working Mother  25
  5  Reflections on Gender  26

**2 Ueda-sensei: Japanese Administrator (1956–1998)**  27
  1  Yamada and Kojima Former Teachers and Colleagues  27
  2  Ueda-Sensei: Teacher, Principal and Community Leader  29

**3 Clare: Home Economics Secondary & Post-Secondary Teacher (1958–1995)**  33
  1  Junior High School Teaching  33
  2  Post-Secondary Teaching  36

4   **Norma: K-16 Teacher (1967–2017)**   41
    1   From Rural Alberta to Urban British Columbia   41
    2   Religion in Schools   43
    3   Special Visits from VIPs: Superintendent and Governor General   44
    4   Discipline   44
    5   Assessment   45

5   **Terry: Nova Scotia/NWT/BC (1971–)**   46
    1   Changes in Curriculum, Teaching and Learning and Special Education   47
    2   Teaching up North in Yellowknife, NWT   49
    3   Changes in Assessment Practices   51

6   **Beverly: Rural Ontario to Europe (1972–2021)**   53
    1   Early Memories as a Novice Teacher   54
    2   Teaching Overseas (Germany, Belgium and the Gulf War)   56

7   **Bill: Secondary PE & Social Studies (1973–2015)**   58
    1   Physical Education as a Pathway to Teaching   58
    2   Changes in Curriculum, Teaching and Learning   59
    3   Changes in Technology   61
    4   Changes in Assessment and Evaluation   61

8   **Anne: Music Teacher, Administrator & Professor (1984–)**   63
    1   Mentor: High School Band Teacher   63
    2   1980s Ontario Schooling: Religion/Class Considerations   64
    3   Novice Teacher Stories of Experience   64
    4   Mentor: Veteran Teacher/Administrator/Principal/Friend   66
    5   Words of Advice for New Teachers   67

9   **Gloria: Rural Colombia to Urban Canada (1988–)**   68
    1   Colombia to the United Kingdom: Escuela Nueva and Early Teaching   68
    2   The United Kingdom to Canada: Opening Doors through Graduate Studies   71

10  **Ted: Transcultural Teacher from Canada to Japan (1989–)**   73
    1   Formal Education: The Road to Teaching and Academia   73
    2   Teaching Abroad for Personal and Professional Growth   75

|     |     |                                                                 |
| --- | --- | --------------------------------------------------------------- |
|     | 3   | Lessons in Collaboration – Teacher-to-Teacher Conversations  76 |
|     | 4   | Educational Philosophy for Integrated Learning  77              |

11 **Vessy: SOGI (Sexual Orientation & Gender Identity) Leader (1996–)**  80
    1    Coaching and Competitive Sports: A Pathway to Teaching  80
    2    Mentoring of Teachers  82
    3    SOGI (Sexual Orientation and Gender Identity) Leadership  82

12 **Alicia: Inclusive Special Education Entrepreneur**  84
    1    Practicum Experience: Sink or Swim?  85
    2    Tutoring Special Needs Students  86
    3    Teaching Social Skills  87

13 **Three Sensei: Novice, Mid-Career & Veteran Teachers**  90
    1    Narrative of Miss Sakaguchi, Novice Teacher  90
    2    Veteran Teacher, Kimura-Sensei's Mentorship of Shimazaki-Sensei  93
    3    A Tribute to Hiro-Sensei, a Mid-Career Teacher  94
    4    Teacher Relationships  96

14 **Mari and Ken: Japan's Next Generation of Teachers**  98
    1    Marathons and High-Stakes Testing in Japan  98
    2    Mari-Sensei's Transcultural Journey  99
    3    Ken-Sensei's Struggle against the Status Quo  102

15 **Carolyn: Sixties Scoop Story of Indigenous Resilience**  104
    1    The Importance of Family and Community  104
    2    Reflections on Indigenizing Our Pedagogies of Practice  106

16 **Marie: Secwépemc Language Teacher**  110
    1    Background  110
    2    Educational Philosophy  113

17 **John: Transformational Teacher from Vietnam to Rural BC**  116
    1    Teaching in Vietnam  117
    2    Teaching in Rural BC  118
    3    Educational Philosophy  120

18    Mrs. Henderson: Northern BC Inner-City School Experience    124
    1    Background and Cultural Context    124
    2    Stories of Resistance and Resilience    125
    3    Challenging Students    126
    4    Challenging Parents: Dealing with Difficult Parents in a Small Community    127
    5    Challenging Times: COVID-19 Trauma and Stress    128
    6    Teaching Philosophy Final Reflections    129

19    Sean: Primary Teacher amidst the COVID-19 Pandemic    131
    1    Educational Philosophy    131
    2    Kindergarten Teacher    134
    3    Challenges of the Pandemic – Working at the Essential Services School    135
    4    Grade 3/4 Split Class    135

20    Glen Hansman: Intermediate Teacher, Former BCTF President & LGBTQ Advocate    137
    1    Challenges of a Novice Teacher in a Changing Political Climate    138
    2    British Columbia Teachers' Federation President Highlights    140
    3    Back in the Classroom: A Look to the Future    141

**Afterword**    143
  *Cheryl Craig*

**Appendix A: Critical Response Questions**    145
**Appendix B: Marie's Journal**    148
**References**    160
**Index**    166

# Foreword

*Ruth Hayhoe*

This book invites the reader into a rich set of narratives by and about teachers across Canada and in Japan. It is comparative in a diachronic sense in that we first hear the stories of teachers whose careers unfolded over the second half of the 20th century, followed by a much younger group of teachers with very different experiences of formation who are dealing with the challenges of teaching in the 21st century right up to the current COVID crisis. It is comparative also in the inclusion of three sets of teacher narratives from the Japanese context which present striking differences from the Canadian context. At the heart of this comparison is the life experience of the author, who grew up in British Columbia, was initially trained as a secondary school teacher of physics and then spent two years teaching in Japan. His doctoral study at OISE, University of Toronto enabled him to develop research involving in-depth comparison between the lives of teachers in Japan and Canada and he finally settled into an academic position in British Columbia, where he has contributed to the formation of many teachers with diverse backgrounds.

In the Prologue and Introduction, Edward (Ted) explains how he learned narrative method in a class with Michael Connelly at OISE, and how interactive groups with fellow students enabled him to experience its richness. He further elaborates on his appreciation of critical ethnography and decision to integrate that within narrative inquiry, giving readers an understanding of his use of the term Teacher Acculturation in this book's title. Then his own narrative illustrates this method, as Chapter 10 among the 20 case studies that fill out the book. I sense the term "portraits" might be an even better way to depict these chapters, each focusing on one or more individual teachers and allowing the reader to hear their stories, largely in their own words, and reflect on their philosophy of education as it played out in their teaching and leadership experience. Among the teacher narratives there is a great diversity, such that readers can feel at a deep level what it has meant to be an immigrant coming into Canada from Colombia, having experienced the progressive influence of *Escuela Nueva*, or how an experience of teaching abroad in Vietnam or Germany influences the teacher acculturation process. Perhaps most moving of all are the stories of Indigenous women who succeeded in overcoming the painful legacy of residential schools and bringing the wealth of their traditional cultural and familial perspectives into classrooms that had long excluded them. The portraits of Japanese teachers of two generations, who faced similar issues in a very different context provide a backdrop to these Canadian portraits.

The book can also be seen as a kind of panorama of the Canadian experience of teaching across the country from Nova Scotia, through Ontario and Quebec, Saskatchewan, and the North, in both rural and urban environments, with the city of Kamloops, British Columbia, where the author has been based at Thompson Rivers University, as a core coming together point. Most important, from my perspective, is the way in which the book embodies the rich features of narrative method as a way of facilitating forms of reciprocal learning and intercultural understanding that are so crucial to achieving sustainability and a lasting peace in our current world. I would place this book in the same league as books in the series *Intercultural Reciprocal Learning in Chinese and Western Education*,[1] edited by Michael Connelly and Shijing Xu, a fellow doctoral student of this author years ago. There is a natural flow to the text and a vividness in the articulation of ideas and experiences that take it far beyond the typical academic text on teacher education and open up vistas of a transformation in the teacher acculturation process.

### Note

1   For a review of this series, see *Frontiers of Education in China*, Vol. 15, No. 3, pp. 526–529.

# Dedication

This book is dedicated to my parents who have supported me throughout my academic journey. My mother encouraged me from a young age to keep a journal and to share stories of experience. Leading by example, Mom documented her own stories and those of other family members, including many of Dad's humourous anecdotes and fascinating adventures. Mom and Dad were my first teachers. Indeed, the first teacher conversations are between a parent and a child. I have learned a great deal from both my mother and father. I hope to pass on some of this wisdom to my own children.

# Acronyms

| | |
|---|---|
| AB | Alberta |
| ADHD | Attention Deficit Hyperactivity Disorder |
| AEST | Ministry of Advanced Education Skills and Training |
| AET | Assistant English Teacher |
| ALT | Assistant Language Teacher |
| BC | British Columbia |
| BCCT | British Columbia College of Teachers |
| BCTF | British Columbia Teachers' Federation |
| BEd | Bachelor of Education |
| BHE | Bachelor of Home Economics |
| BIPOC | Black, Indigenous and people of colour |
| CEN | Comparative Ethnographic Narrative |
| COVID-19 | Coronavirus Disease and Pandemic |
| CP | Canadian Pacific |
| CTL | Curriculum, Teaching, and Learning |
| DEA | Drug Enforcement Administration |
| EAS | Educational Assistants |
| Ec | economics |
| EDI | Equity, Diversity, and Inclusion |
| EFL | English as a Foreign Language |
| ELL | English Language Learners |
| ESL | English as a Second Language |
| FNESC | First Nations Education Steering Committee |
| FTE | full time equivalent |
| ICT | Information and Communications Technology |
| IBL | inquiry-based learning |
| IE | Industrial Education |
| IEP | Individualized Education Plans |
| JICA | Japan International Cooperation Agency |
| K-16 | kindergarten through post-secondary |
| KSD 73 | Kamloops School District 73 |
| LGBTQ | Lesbian, Gay, Bisexual, Transgender, Queer |
| MA | Master of Arts |
| MEd | Master of Education |
| MEXT | Ministry of Education, Sports and Culture (of Japan) |
| NATO | North Atlantic Treaty Organization |
| NWT | Northwest Territories |

| | |
|---|---|
| OCT | Ontario College of Teachers |
| OISE | Ontario Institute for the Studies of Education |
| ON | Ontario |
| PLCS | Professional Learning Communities |
| PhD | Doctor of Philosophy |
| PE | Physical Education |
| PMQS | Private Military Quarters |
| PD | Professional Development |
| PBL | project-based learning |
| SCES | Secwépemc Cultural Education Society |
| SES | Socioeconomic Status |
| SHAPE | Supreme Headquarters of the Allied Powers of Europe |
| SOGI | Sexual Orientation and Gender Identity |
| SSD 36 | Surrey School District 36 |
| S-STTEP | Self-study of teaching and teacher education practices |
| TESOL | Teaching English as an Other Language |
| TOC | Teacher on Call |
| TRU | Thompson Rivers University |
| TTOC | Teacher Teaching on Call |
| TGS | Think, Group, Share |
| TPS | Think, Pair, Share |
| UBC | University of British Columbia |
| UDL | universal design for learning |
| UK | United Kingdom |
| USA | United States of America |
| UT | University of Toronto |
| UVic | University of Victoria |
| VCR | video-tape recorder |
| VESTA | Vancouver Elementary School Teachers' Association |
| VSB | Vancouver School Board |
| WWII | Second World War |

# Guide to the Reader

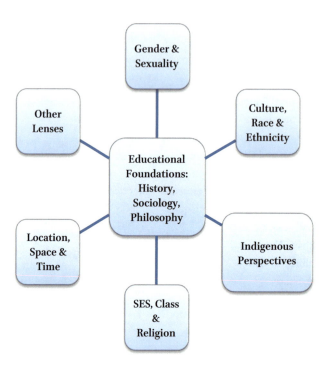

**Educational Foundations Lenses**

This graphic organizer evolved through my teaching of educational foundations classes to teacher candidates. It provides a framework for the teacher stories shared in this book. Moreover, as my teaching and narrative research are inexorably linked, the educational foundations lenses form an integral part of my own teacher acculturation, in concert with the evolution of my thinking and the creation of this book. Through this research, it became clear that teacher acculturation occurs through a kaleidoscope of lenses. Other lenses identified include but are not limited to Equity, Diversity, and Inclusion (EDI) and Curriculum, Teaching, and Learning (CTL). CTL encompasses Assessment, Educational Psychology, Information and Communications Technology (ICT), and major challenges such as Covid-19. Readers are encouraged to expand on these educational foundations lenses and to critically reflect on how these lenses frame our teacher acculturation. Teachers may find the *Teacher Acculturation Matrix* below helpful in identifying which stories illustrate or exemplify each of these educational foundations lenses.

## Teacher Acculturation Matrix

| Educational foundations lens/chapter | Gender & sexuality | Culture, race & ethnicity | SES, class & religion | Indigenous perspectives | Location, space & time (rural/urban) | Other (EDI/ICT/CTL/COVID-19) |
|---|---|---|---|---|---|---|
| 1. Hazel | X | | | | X | |
| 2. Ueda | | X | | | X | |
| 3. Clare | X | X | | | X | |
| 4. Norma | X | | X | | X | |
| 5. Terry | | | X | | X | X |
| 6. Beverly | | | | | X | X |
| 7. Bill | | | | | X | X |
| 8. Anne | | | X | | X | |
| 9. Gloria | | X | | | | |
| 10. Ted | | X | | | | X |
| 11. Vessy | X | | X | | | X |
| 12. Alicia | | | | | | X |
| 13. 3 Sensei | | X | | | | X |
| 14. Mari/Ken | | X | | | | X |
| 15. Carolyn | | | X | X | | X |
| 16. Marie | | | | X | | X |
| 17. John | | X | | | X | X |
| 18. Mrs. H | | | | | X | |
| 19. Sean | | | | | | X |
| 20. Glen | X | | | | | X |

# Prologue

How does one become an effective teacher? The answer to this question can best be found in conversations with teachers. Teaching is something that has been studied by researchers for many years, yet the complex work of teachers remains largely a mystery. There is no definitive guide for how to become a teacher. The most significant lessons for teaching are often learned serendipitously. Fortunately, teachers' personal, practical, and professional experiences provide a rich database of pedagogical knowledge. Mentorship can be critically important in the early years of learning how to teach. Through personal reflection as well as collaboration with teacher colleagues, tacit understandings and wisdom in the practice of teaching can be uncovered and better understood.

*Teacher-to-teacher conversations* (Howe, 2005a, 2005b; Yonemura, 1982) provide a wealth of knowledge. As a former secondary teacher and now as a teacher educator and researcher, I have had hundreds of conversations with other teachers about their early career experiences. During my doctoral research, I pioneered the use of *comparative ethnographic narrative* (CEN) to investigate teacher acculturation (Howe, 2005a, 2005b, 2010). CEN is well-aligned with the self-study of teaching and teacher education practices (S-STTEP) to go beyond storytelling and to facilitate reflexive turns (Bullock & Peercy, 2018; LaBoskey, 2004; Loughran, 2010). CEN is a blend of reflexive ethnography (Etherington, 2006) and narrative inquiry (Clandinin & Connelly, 2000). Essentially, CEN is a collaborative narrative inquiry –*comparative* (as it involves comparing one's experiences with others); *ethnographic* (in situ, long term participant-observation); and *narrative* (incorporating peer to peer extended conversations). It is a form of self-study, joint auto-ethnography or other forms of collaborative, interpretive research (Ellis & Bochner, 2000; Loughran, 2007). CEN unearths fertile, descriptive narrative data. The CEN cyclical process of telling stories, reflecting on stories and re-telling stories with a co-researcher, helps facilitate interpretation and deep analysis, to uncover rich lived experiences.

Through CEN using *teacher-to-teacher conversations*, I have been investigating teacher acculturation for more than two decades. I have collected dozens of stories of experience, highlighting the challenges faced by novice teachers over the past 70 years. More than twenty stories are included here. Each chapter focuses on a particular teacher's story (some chapters include more than one) with lessons for prospective teachers. Thus, this book provides a glimpse into the fascinating journey of becoming a teacher – something I call *teacher acculturation*. While socialization is sometimes used, I feel that the term "acculturation" better encompasses the messy process of becoming a teacher.

It is hoped this book will be of practical use for teacher candidates, teachers, and teacher educators. The *Teacher Acculturation Matrix* (see Guide to the Reader) provides a reader's guide in terms of connections to educational foundations such as gender, sexuality, language, culture, race, ethnicity, class, socioeconomic status, religion, Indigenous perspectives, time, location, space and other lenses. While this book can be used as a textbook in educational foundations, it is hoped that anyone interested in the lives of teachers might be interested in reading these stories, to gain insights into the lives of teachers and how teaching has evolved and changed since the mid-20th century. In addition, teacher educators may find this book useful in teaching history and philosophy of education to teacher candidates and may choose to focus on particular chapters that are most relevant. To facilitate discussion, critical response questions for each chapter are included in Appendix A. I have found an effective way to teach educational foundations is to use a case study approach. Each chapter is in essence a case study. Teacher candidates can do a Think, Pair, Share but as a small group, so I call this Think, Group, Share (Howe & Cope Watson, 2020, 2021). First, I have them think about the questions individually. Then, they work in online groups of three to discuss the questions. I also participate in this discussion. Finally, as an entire class, we discuss the questions together in class. In this way, teacher candidates engage with the readings and are better prepared to actively participate in lively class discussions and debates.

I have found educational chronicles are one of the most effective ways to investigate teaching philosophies and emerging teacher identities of teacher candidates (see Figure 1). An educational chronicle details education and experience, both formal and informal from birth to present day. In conjunction with other narrative tools such as memory boxes, pictures, artifacts, journals and so on, it can help us to frame and articulate our educational philosophy. As a graduate student at OISE/UT in 2001, I was first introduced to educational chronicles and narrative inquiry by Michael Connelly, widely considered a pioneer of narrative inquiry. At that time, I created my first educational chronicle and I have used it as an example in my teaching ever since.

Essentially, my educational chronicle is a timeline that I chose to create in a linear-sequential fashion, but it could easily have been articulated in a more artistic, graphical way as a webpage, mosaic, song, poem or multi-media presentation. Building on the educational chronicle, I have used it as a springboard for teacher candidate group activities to promote conversations about education and experience. I have studied this signature lesson as part of my self-study research (Howe & Cope Watson, 2020). Recently, I have extended this lesson to digital online teaching (Howe & Cope Watson, 2021). The educational chronicle has helped me to remember the most important events along my academic journey.

PROLOGUE 3

## Ted's Educational Chronicle 1966–2021

**Life Events**

- parental support to learn to read
- honour roll and intrinsic motivation to learn (grade 3–)
- swimming, sailing, Pender Island, family and life-long friendships
- Academic/Citizenship awards (grade 7)
- Europe band tour 1982/lived with grandmother (1983)
- UBC residence, tutoring
- developed personal hobbies & interests
- Japan (1990–1992)
- travel/professional development
- married E (1992), separated (2014), met L (2016), divorced E (2018)
- children born: J (1998), M (2002), S (2006)
- Japan for PhD research (2002–2005)
- university teaching and research in Japan
- tsunami (2011)
- Kamloops, BC

**Formal Educational Events**

(Age) 5, 10, 15, 20, 25, 30, 35, 40, 45, 50

- piano/clarinet/band
- influential elementary school teachers
- Science fair (grade 7)
- learned to drive (age 16)
- hated high school English
- failed Math 100 (score: 36/75)
- liked English Composition
- BSc (Physics, 1988). Decided to become a teacher.
- BEd (Secondary Science, 1992)
- MA Thesis/UBC Educational Studies
- MA (2000)
- OISE/UT (2001–2005)
- PhD (2005)
- Assistant Professor
- Tenure
- Assoc. Prof. (2017)

FIGURE 1   Educational chronicle example

To introduce CEN and to provide a framework for the other teacher stories within this book, I have included my own stories of experience and education (see also Chapter 10). Here, I have chosen six exceptional experiences spanning my academic lifetime to illustrate the close connection between experience and education that has become an essential component of my CEN and this book. The first story exemplifies the importance of parental support for a grade 1 student as risk of failing. I owe my love of reading to my parents' and teachers' support and continued encouragement. The second story involves my grade 6 and 7 teachers' appreciation of my creative and descriptive writing. As a result, I became an avid writer. The third story details my grade 7 science fair experience. This event precipitated my love of learning and research. In contrast, the fourth story is a negative one involving analysis of literature and expository writing in high school. Subsequently, I became disinterested in language arts. However, this experience taught me it is the way in which curriculum is taught rather than the content that has a greater influence on students. The fifth anecdote occurred during my fourth year of undergraduate studies while taking a writing course. It was then that I learned the importance of being clear and concise. The final incident occurred while studying Japanese. As a result, I learned empathy for children experiencing difficulty in learning. It is hoped that through the analysis and interpretation of these six illustrative stories it will become clear how educational chronicles can be used to unearth teachers' personal practical knowledge. Also, this illustrates how CEN works as a research methodology.

1      Learning to Read: The Importance of Support from Home

In grade 1, around the fourth week of school mom received a phone call from my teacher saying, "Ted refuses to open his reader. He has been put in the 'slow-learners' group." Apparently, I wasn't the least bit interested in reading, despite my parents' shared reading of nursery rhymes and other children's literature. My mother insisted that I was not a 'slow-learner' and she resolved to do all she could to get me reading. Her encouragement included weekly trips to the library where I would choose books (with a little help and guidance from my mom) that were to my liking. In a short time, I was out of the slow reading group. Moreover, by the end of grade 1, I was one of the most promising students in the top-learning group. I became an honour roll student and eventually won several of the top academic awards at my elementary school. My parents' support had a great deal to do with my love of reading, my love of learning and my academic success.

This incident exemplifies the dangers of labeling a child and the problems inherent with streaming. Perhaps if it were not for my parents' support, I may have been labeled a 'slow-learner' and 'under-achiever.' Indeed, this situation could have led to a self-defeating prophesy where I would have become convinced that I was not a good student and was incapable of doing well. Thank goodness for my positive home environment.

As a teacher this incident has affected me profoundly. I try to avoid labeling students and I routinely group students heterogeneously. Although I have compassion for the students that are English as a Foreign Language (EFL), English as a Second Language (ESL) or *Special Needs* (mentally or physically challenged), I do not give them special treatment. I believe it is in their best interest if they can be included in as many class activities as possible. I encourage all students to think for themselves and to work together. Before asking me a question, I would like them to have first read their textbook/handout, checked the glossary/notes and asked their partner. The teacher can try to help each student one on one but to reach all students in this way is nearly impossible. There is no substitute for a caring parent. I know that not every student will have the ideal home learning environment, however. I have come to respect the support of some parents and to be critical of others. The effect of the parents and the home cannot be overstated.

## 2      Learning to Write: The Significance of Teachers

In grades 6 and 7, I had two outstanding teachers. Through their efforts I began to love writing. The various projects allowed me to express myself in many different ways. I was introduced to scientific writing in the form of lab reports and research for my science fair project. I wrote short stories and did an autobiography as well as reports on things that were really interesting to me. I kept a diary at this time. I wrote letters to pen pals. I wrote thank-you notes to relatives. I even wrote lengthy notes to other classmates that were of a personal nature. My grade 6 and 7 teachers made all these activities possible. In particular, I most enjoyed creative writing. In my grade 7 class we shared our writing with the other students on a regular basis. I was very proud of my work and I enjoyed reading it to the other students. I have kept much of my writing including my autobiography from this class and to this day it still gives me a great deal of pleasure reading it.

Reflecting on this experience – I realize how special the teacher-student relationship is and how important writing is in all aspects of education. I have encouraged my students to write in journals and to do creative writing as well as scientific writing. Written language was an integral part of my science classroom including a 'Science News' bulletin board, science concept maps, cartoons, 'Today's Agenda' and examples of student's written work. I have always tried to motivate students to do their very best and to take pride in their work.

## 3    Learning to Research: Finding a Niche for a Life's Work

One of the most significant things that happened to me in school was the grade 7 science fair. While I don't have much memory of the things we did in science class, the science fair left a lasting impression on me. It was something that happened mostly outside of school. It was a self-directed endeavor. Of course, with this sort of open-ended unsupervised project, you get everything from 'what kind of gum has the best flavour' to my friend's astronomy research. He was an amateur astronomer with over three years of data collected. It is hard to compete with that! He came in first, while I came in second.

My study was on plant nutrition. My hypothesis was to prove that plants needed water, sunlight and nutrients to grow. It seemed logical that the more nutrients a plant receives the better it would grow. With Dad's help and guidance, I planted green beans in about 40 pots, filled with vermiculite and soil. I had control plants with water and sunlight while my variable was the type of fertilizer. I had four different kinds of plant fertilizer: (1) allpurpose blend of 20-20-20 nitrogen/phosphorus/potassium; (2) nitrogen; (3) phosphorus; and (4) potassium. Every day I carefully observed the bean plants, meticulously drew detailed diagrams, measured their growth to the nearest millimeter and plotted their progress on a broken line graph. It was quite an ambitious project for a grade 7 student, but I had some help getting started from my dad. Once I knew what to do, I was on my way. I really liked collecting and analyzing data and producing the highest quality report. I felt very important. However, something went horribly wrong. Many of my plants died! I thought I was doing the right thing. I was watering them every day, watching them carefully and making sure they all got plenty of light. Nevertheless, the nitrogen beans barely grew at all, while the beans that had just water and sunlight (the control group) grew much better. At the time, I thought, I'm not going to do very well in the science fair. I killed half my plants! My hypothesis wasn't proved correct. I had thought giving lots of nutrients would be better for the plants, however, I didn't know how much to give and too much of a nutrient can seriously harm the growth of a plant.

I learned something special from this experience – scientists rarely prove a hypothesis. Often from their experiments, researchers learn something new, something entirely different from their hypothesis and further questions come out of that.

The science fair was a key event in my life. That alone got me interested in science and research. It acted as a catalyst to encourage me to continue studying, learning and asking further questions. This led me to become a physics teacher and eventually a social scientist. As I think back on what I did then and what gives me satisfaction in my career now, I see a strong connection.

## 4  Traditional Didactic Teaching: The Antithesis of My Teaching Philosophy

My fond memories of elementary school language education compare sharply with my experience in high school. By the time I had reached grade 11, I thoroughly disliked English. The joy I had experienced doing creative writing had been replaced by the clinical, impersonal expository and précis writing associated with the analysis of literature. I began to really hate my English teacher! He was so old fashioned and set in his ways. We sat in alphabetical order and he used to embarrass us by calling on us to answer questions if we were not paying attention. A lack of freedom and a total absence of creativity and personal choice characterize my memories of high school English. Everyone had to read Shakespeare's great works and various other classics. It was good in a sense, that we were exposed to such authors as John Steinbeck (whom I became quite a fan of), but I feel that we needed some variety in the choice of literature. If a student likes Steinbeck's work, why can't he read several of Steinbeck's novels instead of all the prescribed readings of the curriculum. Students have to feel some kind of connection to what they read. It has to be relevant to them. I rarely felt very passionate about the books I was forced to read and as such many of my essays lacked a critical analysis and were quite dry and boring. Herein lies the problem with traditional approaches to language education and literature. Students must be given a variety of experiences that will turn them on to reading and writing about literature. All kinds of 'real' reading and writing should be encouraged in all language classrooms, all the way through high school. Why abandon creative writing and only focus on expository writing? Students need to practice all forms of written expression.

My own high school experience has helped my teaching immensely. I try to incorporate a variety of teaching strategies to engage the students. I also regularly give students the opportunity to make choices. For example, in my Physics 11 class I encouraged each student to choose a topic for a research paper that interests them. Students presented their findings to the class. In this way, in addition to the formal written research paper, students had the opportunity to explain the concept in their own words so that everyone may share in their discoveries. This example serves to illustrate a fundamental belief I hold – written expression and communication are important cross-curricular goals. Using a variety of teaching strategies is essential for realizing these and other goals.

## 5  Learning to Enjoy Writing Again: An Undergraduate Transformation

It wasn't until fourth year university that I entertained the thought of becoming a teacher and it was then that I enrolled in English 303 Written Composition.

At the time, my immediate objective was to enhance my chances of being accepted to the faculty of education. It had been several years since I had written anything other than lab reports, so I was a little intimidated by the experienced essay writers (arts majors) that formed the majority of the class. I was pleasantly surprised however when the professor explained that we would be delving into all forms of essay writing, including creative and descriptive writing! I was so happy to be given the chance to choose my own essay topics and to write about things that mattered to me. It had been many years since I had experienced this positive feeling toward writing. Indeed, I had the impression that these forms of writing were limited to the elementary classroom. In any case, I quickly got over the euphoria when my first essay was returned to me. Apparently, my writing had not yet fully evolved from my high school efforts to the academic caliber of a university undergraduate student. I still had some lessons to be learned.

I learned that in order to be an effective writer, one must be clear and concise while avoiding redundancy. I learned that quantity must never be mistaken for quality. I believe this has shaped my thinking in a dramatic way. In fact, my philosophical nature is one that values quality work from myself and from my students. I also try to be clear and concise in my own teaching including speaking as well as writing. These guiding principles were introduced in English 303 and were later revisited in my education classes. Recently, in my writing I have reconfirmed the importance of doing quality work as well as being clear and concise. Moreover, in teaching, being clear was especially important with the abundance of ESL and *at risk* students in my classes.

Having taught for a number of years, I have gained some insights about some effective teaching strategies for EFL, ESL and 'at risk' students but it is from another experience that I have gained empathy for these children. During a two-year leave of absence (1990–1992), I lived in Tokyo, Japan and taught English at the junior high school level. I came to realize that 'at risk' students received little or no help. They were simply promoted from year to year and were not expected to participate in the class activities. I remember asking one grade 9 student who had studied English for three years, "What's your name?" ... He was unable to respond. This student could not even spell his name in English after three years of language instruction. The education system in Canada appears to do a much better job of catering to the individual needs of these special students. However, do Canadian teachers perhaps cater too much by expecting less of them? If teachers expect little or nothing, that is exactly what they get. I believe that on the contrary we must expect more. If we raise our expectations, students should rise to the challenge, provided we offer them continued encouragement and support.

## 6 Learning a Foreign Language in an Immersion Classroom

I have chosen an experience that has shaped my teaching in a very direct and personal way. Here I recount my brief stint (March–June, 1992) as a student in a Japanese Immersion classroom.

> *It is a crisp spring day. The cherry blossoms are about to bloom, and the noonday sun is streaming through the crowded spaces and reflecting off the glass and concrete office towers of Shinjuku. As the train comes to a halt I check the station sign – Sendagaya, yes that's right. I grab my knapsack and get off. As I head down the stairs, across the street to the large ominous building with the intimidating "Sendagaya Foreign Language Institute" sign, I am struck by the fact that I'm nervous and anxious. Why? Well, I deliberately over-estimated my Japanese language ability in order to get into this pilot study language class… but how fluent is an 'intermediate student' anyway? Now I am about to find out. I enter the building, take the elevator up to the sixth floor where I am directed to a small, sparsely decorated classroom, dominated by a chalkboard and desk at the front. It is typical except for one feature – there are about 12 chairs arranged in a semi-circle facing the front. Many of the students are already present. "Konnichi-wa, Dozo, haite, kudasai!" says a middle-aged woman I presume to be our sensei. I respond with a cautious, "Hai" and with a bow of my head I enter the room. It is quite a multicultural group as we discover in the introductions… entirely in Japanese. I am overwhelmed! Now I know what is meant by immersion. The whole class is in Japanese. No English is used. Suddenly, I am no longer the 'super-keener.' The tables have been turned. I shrink into my seat when a question is asked. I am afraid of making a mistake. I feel way out of my league. Everyone seems so confident! I now fully relate to the* ESL *experience.*

While this was many years ago, the memories are deeply embedded in my psyche. The pictures are visual, but the emotions and feelings are far stronger and more vivid. I can barely recall the classroom features or the other people, yet I remember the significant effect this had on my teaching. I have a great deal more empathy for EFL students now that I have experienced their helplessness in a foreign classroom. I have a more comprehensive understanding of EFL, ESL and *at risk* students because of my experience in Japan. In a way, I was an *at risk* student or at least the Japanese foreign language equivalent of an ESL student in one of our classes in Canada. For the first time in my life, I felt the fear of making a mistake or of raising my hand to volunteer information. At times I was totally confused and had difficulty doing what the teacher asked of me. As an adult, I was able to cope and of course there were other adult students who were also struggling, so I can really see how EFL students in my classes now would have much more difficulty in coping.

From my experiences in the Canadian and Japanese school systems, I have learned many important things that have influenced me as a teacher. The six striking incidents I have described have each contributed to my own educational, philosophy and my principles of teaching, which can be summed up with the ancient Chinese proverb also articulated by Dewey (1938):

*I hear – I forget,*
*I see – I remember,*
*I do – I understand.*

I believe that the home environment and the support of both teachers and parents play an important role in education. In addition, students must be encouraged to strive to do their very best quality work. As teachers we must set a good example by being clear and concise in our own writing. We must let students know that we value quality work. While we should have empathy for all students, regardless of whether the student is EFL, ESL or *at risk*, we should still expect each student to work to their utmost potential and to exhibit a sense of accomplishment and pride in their work. I have frequently used student presentations, group work, peer evaluation and portfolio assessment in my teaching, reflecting my strong belief in quality over quantity. By having students select their very best work at the end of the year for their portfolios, they go back and review and reflect on the material learned previously. A portfolio can be used as a sort of memory box for their ideas or a time capsule to be opened in the future.

## 7   Memory Box: Stories from a Teacher's Briefcase

I keep a *memory box*. Inside I store photos and other artifacts. In addition, I have kept scrapbooks, journals, diaries and I have an extensive collection of home movies as well as other memorabilia such as letters, a baby book and the like. These things help me recall events in my past. One of my best examples of a *memory box* is a scrapbook of my stay in Japan from 1990–1992. I kept receipts, train fares, postcards and other everyday objects to remind me of my experiences. It is surprising to see photos of rows of public phones and hundreds of bicycles parked around Shinjuku station. It is easy to forget this was how it was like for me commuting to my job as an Assistant English Teacher then at Yodobashi 2nd Junior Highschool (now a community centre, as families have moved out of Shinjuku to the suburbs).

There is only one *memory box* that has followed me on my journey through teaching. It is my briefcase – a graduation gift from my grandmother, it has been by my side since 1989. A handsome, large, soft, black leather case that cost nearly $300 that I am so proud of. It has weathered well but it is showing its age. Several times I have spent considerable money repairing the handle and seams. I wouldn't trade it as it has such sentimental value. Every day, it would accompany me to school/work. Inside the briefcase, I have kept my teaching daybook and all the necessary tools of the profession. If this briefcase could talk it would tell some great stories chronicling my career:

> *(1) September 1990, Tokyo, Japan. My handle broke! He should take better care of me. What was he thinking stuffing me full of all that carry-on luggage? I am a briefcase not a suitcase! In any case (pun intended), I am at this fancy office and we are greeted by an extremely courteous receptionist. Soon, two men in lab coats appear and whisk me away. Within minutes, I have a brand new handle with beautiful gold rivets. No charge! This is Japanese full service for you!*

> *(2) Friday October 13, 2000. Thesis deadline. The MA thesis is 113 pages and there will be 13 hardbound copies... it is a good thing my owner is not superstitious. The time is 12 midnight. What am I doing carrying this document around at this ungodly hour? We have school tomorrow! Thank goodness, Kinko's is open 24 hours. Why? Because there is a mistake in Figure 7 (the colour stacked bar graph) ... Japan and British Columbia have been switched! So, here we are literally at the eleventh hour desperately trying to fix this graphic. The computer at Kinko's won't cooperate! What You See Is not necessarily What You Get! Finally, after nearly 1 hour and several different computers later p. 69 Fig. 7 is carefully inserted into the thesis and the original document is complete, safe and secure inside a plastic wrapping within me.*

One of my most precious memory box treasures, along with my briefcase, are the diaries and journals I have kept since childhood. I have found a reflective journal an effective tool in both teaching and research. I encourage all teachers to keep a journal as it is an excellent way to remember and to recall lessons. For readers keen to catch of glimpse of a first-year teacher's reflexive journal writing, please see Marie's example in Appendix B.

INTRODUCTION

# Comparative Ethnographic Narrative

I entered my doctoral studies with a clear idea of what I wanted to research and how I wanted to go about it – or so I thought. While my MA had been highly quantitative, I decided a qualitative approach was necessary to investigate the contested and messy world of teacher acculturation. Reflexive ethnography seemed like the best way to study the transition from student to teacher. However, one course, with one professor, changed my way of thinking entirely. Serendipity played a major role in what transpired. As a graduate student at the Ontario Institute for Studies in Education/University of Toronto (OISE/UT), I had to select from a number of curriculum studies sections offered. I chose Michael Connelly's section because of our shared background in science education and the fact it suited my schedule. At that time, I knew nothing of Professor Connelly's pioneering work and extensive scholarship in narrative inquiry. Our first class was held on September 11, 2001 at 9:00 am. Of course, there is a lot more I could say about that fateful day but suffice to say, it was a day that profoundly changed the lives of many people, including the twelve students in this class. In terms of my curriculum, teaching and learning, Mick Connelly opened my eyes to the significance of teachers' personal, practical knowledge, professional knowledge landscape, and the power of narrative inquiry (Clandinin & Connelly, 2000).

   At first, ethnography was my chosen research methodology as I intended to spend a long time in the field. My rationale was that this approach would best provide rich, detailed descriptions and practical knowledge for improving teacher induction. It was only through subsequent coursework, I chose to blend elements of narrative inquiry, in order to more fully investigate teacher acculturation. Through a number of reflective processes, my own personal, professional and practical knowledge of curriculum, teaching and learning was unearthed. These activities included writing letters; making journal entries; telling personal and family stories; using metaphors, picturing exercises and a memory box; drafting an educational chronicle; producing a teacher conversational interview; and collaborating on group assignments with other students. As the course progressed, increasingly I saw the relevance of how I became a teacher to my own research, through the interconnected nature of our class activities. Ultimately, this cumulative process of recovery and reconstruction of meaning assisted me in composing my teaching narrative.

Subsequently, I revised my research plan, integrating narrative inquiry with reflexive ethnography to investigate Japan's teacher acculturation. I wanted to do a critical study, but I knew this would be challenging, despite my two years of experience in Japan and my extensive connections. I enrolled in a critical ethnography course, but I was told that narrative folks didn't mix well with critical ethnographers. So, my supervisor suggested directed studies where I researched how to blend reflexive ethnography with narrative inquiry. The result of this was a change in my research plans and a paper for my comprehensive exam that later evolved into a book chapter focused on *comparative ethnographic narrative* (CEN) in memory of my supervisor who passed away shortly after I completed my PhD (Howe, 2010). CEN is a collaborative form of narrative inquiry. It is similar to self-study, joint auto-ethnography and other forms of collaborative, interpretive research (Ellis & Bochner, 2000; Loughran, 2007). My dissertation described CEN in its early stages (Howe, 2005a, 2005b). CEN provides a conceptual framework for this book on teacher acculturation. Thus, what follows is a brief description of CEN, which is something that has evolved over the past two decades, from my doctoral research, through my recent self-study research and culminating in this book.

1    Teacher-to-Teacher Conversations

Initial semi-structured interviews and a survey of over 130 teachers were inconclusive as the questions elicited limited responses (Howe, 2000). The survey data seemed to add voices to back up the interview data but provided little new information. However, significantly more was learned in subsequent *teacher-to-teacher conversations* (Howe, 2005a, 2005b) focusing on the same questions. These informal discussions with teachers are better described as *conversations* rather than *interviews* as they included another co-researcher/teacher, fluent in Japanese. Furthermore, the conversations took place over lunch, dinner, or a cup of tea in a relaxed and familiar atmosphere, putting the teachers at ease. The few conversations I had at schools tended to be much more stifling and rigid experiences. Teachers indicated they couldn't open up to me in the same way they could in more comfortable places outside the prying eyes and ears of their administrators and curious colleagues.

   Critical to obtaining reliable data from teachers was making initial contact, then establishing trust and developing rapport. This was a time-consuming and difficult process that was only made possible by a go-between. Personal introductions from mutual friends or acquaintances were essential. Data was obtained from conversations with over 50 teachers. Included were first year teachers, second year teachers, teachers in the middle of their careers, veteran master teachers, administrators, and supervisors as well as retired teachers.

Through CEN, I experienced teachers' daily routines; their interactions with students, teachers, administrators, and parents; and their professional development. Field notes, email exchanges and a personal electronic journal were used to document my experiences and the narratives of the teachers. At the end of each day of participant observation, I de-briefed with a co-researcher before documenting reflections in my electronic journal. This process continued for eight months in conjunction with email contributions from teachers. I met with teachers on a number of occasions for feedback, clarification and to ensure their voices were adequately represented. It prompted me to reflect deeply on my own teaching philosophy:

> As teaching is largely a cultural activity, learning to teach cannot be explained merely by the formal mechanisms of teacher induction programs, or through document review alone. Informal, "behind the scenes" glimpses at teaching provide a more comprehensive view of teacher acculturation. Thus, I use the term *acculturation* rather than *induction*. Moreover, acculturation seems to better capture the personal and serendipitous journey of becoming a teacher, rather than the conventional sociological and anthropological terms, *socialization* or *enculturation*. In my view, teachers aren't *socialized* into the profession, nor are they moulded into professionals through the efforts of other members of the teaching community. Learning to teach is a far more personal endeavour. (Howe, 2010, p. 101)

## 2    Teacher Educator-to-Teacher Educator Conversations

Learning to conduct educational research can be a highly personal endeavour. Many research methodologies, ways of knowing, or theoretical frameworks don't always make sense, nor do they resonate with scholar-practitioners. Noteworthy exceptions – narrative inquiry and reflexive ethnography seem natural to me. As a teacher educator, I have been using narrative inquiry and reflexive ethnography in my teaching and research for well over a decade. In addition, I continue to draw on my personal practical knowledge and professional knowledge landscape, as a teacher for more than 30 years and a transcultural teacher educator, as well as various comparative education experiences. Thus, CEN has evolved into my own personal way of knowing. In the next section, I delve more deeply into the evolution of my CEN conceptual framework and delineate the work of other narrative researchers that have influenced my thinking.

## 3  Evolution of a Teacher Educator's Conceptual Framework

The CEN conceptual framework draws on more than a decade of cross-cultural research (Howe, 2009; Howe & Arimoto, 2014). Employing interviews, surveys, email exchanges, journal writing, and extended conversations, interpretive data has been collected in a number of studies from students, teachers and teacher educators to investigate lived experiences.

Narrative inquiry has become a vital part of my conceptual framework and takes precedence over reflexive ethnography in my research these days. From the onset of my graduate work, Dewey (1938) and the groundbreaking work of Connelly and Clandinin (1988) have greatly influenced my thinking. Moreover, from my early years as a teacher, my classroom routines drew from Dewey's notion of education being essentially active reflection on lived experience. Furthermore, Schwab's (1983) practical conception of curriculum grounded in four commonplaces: teacher, learner, subject matter and milieu, also strikes a chord with me as a practitioner. In addition, international narrative inquiry scholarship highlighting the importance of cultural context, nurtures my evolving narrative conceptual framework (Elbaz-Luwisch, 2010; Trahar, 2011). Specifically, following in the tradition of Canadian pioneers in this method (Clandinin, 2007; Clandinin & Connelly, 2000), as a teacher educator I continue to use narrative inquiry in both my teaching and research. Narrative research collaborations have become a seminal part of my work (see for example, Howe & Arimoto, 2014; Howe & Xu, 2013). Without a doubt, narrative research methodologies are in use by a growing number of Canadian scholars (Ciuffetelli Parker, 2011; Huber et al., 2013; Pinnegar & Daynes, 2007). It is noteworthy that narrative has been reflected by recent contributions to the 40th anniversary edition of the Journal of Education for Teaching (Bullough, 2014; Gilroy, 2014; Zeichner, 2014).

In addition, CEN reflects other international sources (Chan & Ng, 2012; Coulter et al., 2007; Latta & Kim, 2011; Rodriguez, 2011). Moreover, the significance of narrative inquiry to teacher education is well known by narrative scholars (Craig, 2011). However, few studies have been conducted outside Western contexts or in the field of comparative and international education (Howe & Xu, 2013). This is something that makes my work unique, as there are few narrative scholars doing work in both teacher education and comparative and international education. A noteworthy exception is the work of Kim Etherington (2006) in the UK.

Self-study of teaching and teacher education is also relevant to narrative inquiry (Kitchen, 2009; Kosnik & Beck, 2010; Loughran et al., 2004). Craig (2008) eloquently pointed out the origins of self-study in the seminal work of Joseph Schwab. Indeed, self-study has proven a natural fit for teacher educators (Loughran, 2007). For instance, transcultural work with teacher candidates shows the implications of self-study and narrative inquiry within preservice teacher education (Xu, 2011; Xu & Connelly, 2009). Furthermore, Adler's (2011) narrative research into her bi-cultural Japanese-American identity resonates with my sense of self-study and narrative pedagogy as a teacher educator outside the mainstream discourse. Another salient example is Iftody's (2013) narrative self-study, drawing on a poststructuralist understanding of identity, within the context of English teacher education. Finally, the closest narrative work to CEN I have found is Ciuffetelli Parker's (2011) "literacy narratives," helping to build teacher candidates' capacity to use their own knowledge as a frame of reference to better understand others' experiences and to reconcile the theory-practice divide. While Ciuffetelli Parker uses triads of teacher education students, I employ pairs of researchers. The important point is that through these sorts of narrative methods, we become curriculum makers (Clandinin & Connelly, 1992; Craig & Ross, 2008), co-constructing knowledge. Thus, teacher educators can become curriculum makers alongside preservice and inservice teachers. This is one goal in promoting narrative pedagogies.

Individuals can recover and reconstruct personal practical knowledge (Clandinin, 1986) through an exploration of "images, personal philosophies, rules, practical principles, rhythms, metaphors and narrative unity" (Connelly & Clandinin, 1988, p. 59). Knowledge is a narrative construct, which references the totality of a person's personal practical knowledge gained from formal and informal educational experience (Xu & Connelly, 2009, p. 221). Naturally, teachers and students use storytelling in their personal and professional lives. Thus, it is an integral part of my curriculum, teaching and learning. The methodology used in the collaborative research of CEN builds on extensive experience. Through CEN, I have uncovered significant insights into the lives of students and teachers.

My research methodology has evolved as I have applied CEN to a variety of situations and then critically reflected on the process. In addition, newer technology has played a significant role in my approach. An iPad has replaced my field journal, iPod, 35 mm camera and video camera. The iPad can be used rather unobtrusively in a way a video camera cannot. Furthermore, one person can focus on using the iPad to make an audio recording, take notes and take pictures or video if necessary while the other can give their full attention to the conversation at hand. These roles can easily be switched during an interview. It is noteworthy that despite the new technology being used, there is still a clear distinction between field text and research text. My field journal and raw data reside in an iPad while my research text is in a PC or laptop. The iPad can be used to easily digitally record conversations, to take pictures and to make notes. Some applications can do all three of these tasks in one. Rather than transcribing word for word from the transcripts, it is reflected on by co-researchers immediately following an interview. Next, the main points are extracted and noted before exporting to a computer. This entire process is done, not individually but with another co-researcher. In my doctoral research it was *teacher-to-teacher conversations*. Later it was *teacher educator-to-teacher educator conversations* (Howe & Arimoto, 2014; Howe & Xu, 2013). In further research, I have utilized *student-to-student conversations* where two international graduate students have focused conversations with their peers. A traditional structured interview with a participant fielding questions from a researcher resembles a one-sided serve and volley tennis match with points quickly earned, as we move from question to question. I prefer to think of CEN as more of an extended rally, which is a lot more meaningful and fun!

## 4    Summary

In this book, I am a co-researcher with the teachers and with a few noteworthy exceptions (Terry, Carolyn, educational philosophy statements from John, Marie, Mrs. H. and Sean). I am the sole-author and narrator. But it is the teacher stories, told mostly in their own words, that is the focus. I have deliberately chosen not to frame each of these stories with my own interpretation and analysis but to rather let readers come to their own conclusions. I prefer not to micro-manage your thinking. *Thus, I invite readers to also be co-researchers, to act as critical friends and to engage in the conversation by reflecting on the questions posed (see Appendix A). Furthermore, I challenge you to pose new questions for discussion. How do these stories resonate with your own education and experience? The CEN cyclical process of telling stories, reflecting on stories, and re-telling stories with co-researchers, helps facilitate interpretation and deep analysis of stories to uncover rich, lived experiences.*

This book illustrates the CEN approach using teacher stories from two different cultural contexts: Japan and Canada. While each of the teacher stories presented in this book, from various cultural contexts, from veterans to neophytes, are unique, there are certain themes that transcend the physical boundaries of time and place. It is interesting to compare and contrast Japan's teachers with Canada's teachers. Japan's teacher acculturation is (and has been) characterized by teacher relationships. These relationships with colleagues, *sempai* (seniors) and *kohai* (juniors) as well as students and parents are critical to the effective acculturation of Japan's teachers. In particular, the recurring themes of *kenshû* (preservice and in-service training or professional development) and *shido* (guidance) provide a mirror for us to reflect on our own teacher acculturation. Teacher relationships and other themes will be further investigated in each of the chapters focused on teachers in Canada, Japan and elsewhere. The teacher stories are arranged chronologically from the 1950s through the 2020s. Included are teachers from all grade levels ranging from kindergarten through university (K-16).

Finally, I wish to point out the importance of capturing oral histories, speaking to elders, parents, grandparents, and others while you can. During the writing of this book, Hazel, a life-long friend and former teacher-colleague of my mother, passed away (see Chapter 1). A little over a year after our *teacher-to-teacher conversation*, I received a phone call from her son, asking if I had a recording of the interview with his mother's stories, as he did not have any recordings to share with his children. Fortunately, I was able to share the recording of our interview in February 2020, made just prior to COVID-19. So, readers, I implore you to please talk to your loved ones and listen to their stories of experience. Record them. Write them down. Cherish them. Share them with others. That is what this book is all about.

CHAPTER 1

# Hazel: Chinese-Canadian Home Economics Teacher (1949–1984)

### 1       The Journey to Becoming a Teacher

Mrs. C. (Hazel) was born and raised in Vernon, BC. Her father and mother were both ethnic Chinese, but her mother was born in Yale, BC, so while self-described as Chinese, Mrs. C. is actually a second generation Canadian. Like many other Chinese labourers at this time, her father came to Canada to work on the CP Rail line for a paltry 50 cents a day while her mother managed to somehow make this modest wage support a large family. As Mrs. C. said, "She could make a silk purse out of a sow's ear. She was too proud to ask for welfare." The youngest of thirteen children, she grew up well below the poverty line. Mrs. C. fell into teaching as many do. It was not her dream to be a teacher, but teaching provided a financial stepping-stone for her future in an era when women and ethnic minorities faced many hurdles. Mrs. C. reminded me that "the Chinese didn't get the vote until 1947" and this was merely two years before she started her teaching career. When interviewed in February of 2020, at age 90, she was readily able to recall her early years as a novice teacher. Her story of lived experience is one of resilience and success.

Mrs. C. started her teaching career in 1949 at the tender age of 20 and retired in 1984. Her brother attended Normal School in the 1930s but as an ethnic Chinese was unable to obtain a teaching job. As noted by Mrs. C.,

> Up until 1947, before the Chinese people got the vote, whether you were a doctor, lawyer or Indian Chief, you couldn't practice the profession. So, teaching in 1949 was just 2 years after we were given the title of full Canadian citizens. I was working at the Bank of Montreal as a summer relief and at the and at the end of the year they said to me, 'we'd like you to be a permanent staff. Would you like to join us?' And I said, "sure" but by this time I had met a lot of Chinese girls who finished grade 12, two years before… the same age, but they were out working and with the salary they got, they were dressed impeccably. I had ankle socks, a Burberry coat and 2 cashmere sweaters and one skirt… and but anyway, so I said, "OK – I'll work… Sign me up! If you'll take me, I don't really need the UBC experience anymore. I'll work at the Bank." So, they typed all the papers for me to sign. I signed everything

except the bonding paper. I signed everything on a Tuesday. And the last paper I had to sign was a paper for the bonding service, to make sure if I absconded with money, they would be reimbursed... Anyway, for some reason, I said to them, "I've signed so many papers today, you can't have my autograph until Thursday." And they were like, "Come on!" No-no... And then on Wednesday, a telegram came from the Armstrong School District, asking... Oh, the Bank was offering me $980 per annum. PER ANNUM! You get that daily, almost! Anyway, I get a telegram at the Bank from the Armstrong School District saying that they needed a substitute, that they needed a teacher for Home Ec. grades 8 to 12... to cover a mat[ernity] leave. And they were willing to pay $1620 per annum. Well, look at 980 and 1620... There was more money, more skirts and more shoes I could buy! So, immediately, I said to the Bank, "sorry, but I think I'm going to take the bigger offer.

Now, this was almost at the beginning of August. And towards the middle of August, I met the Provincial Supervisor of Home Economics in Victoria. I met her at the Hotel Vancouver for tea, she gave me the course of study, on a Saturday and on Tuesday, which is 3 days later, after Labour Day, I had to go out and teach grade 8 to 12 Foods and Clothing, with only 2 years Home Ec[onomics]... No teacher training... nothing! But the whole underlying factor was that [my] they found my name from my Home Ec. teacher in Vernon. And she said, 'I've got a student but she's only in second year of Home Ec. but if she takes the job, I'll be her mentor... Armstrong is only 22 miles from Vernon... I'll mentor her.' "But I had only 3 days to look at the course of study from grades 8 to 12 Foods and Clothing, by myself. And that is how I got started... Only because $1620 per annum was a heck of a lot more money than $980. Had I signed all the papers at the Bank on Tuesday, that opportunity wouldn't have risen. I would have been a Bank of Montreal person, the next 30 years. But something steered me into [teaching]. I had no idea I wanted to be a teacher.

I had no idea I was going to go to UBC [The University of British Columbia]. I came out to Vancouver to visit my married sisters in Vancouver, after grade 12. And at a dinner they said to me, 'What are you going to do now that you're finished grade 12?' I said, "Well, I don't have any money... So, I guess I just stay in Vernon and get my senior matric[ulation]. At least that is one more year of education." And my brother had a grocery store. I can work in the grocery store... And my three married sisters said to me, 'You know, we never had a chance to go further than grade 10, because of poverty... And you're the last one in the family... We would like you to go to UBC... and what we'll do is we'll pass the hat around and we'll each contribute money for the fees.' And each one of the married sisters had their own home in Vancouver and there were no children... 'You can stay with any one of us for free.' Free room and board. That's how I went to UBC. I had no idea of going to UBC. I had no idea of becoming a teacher. So, somehow circumstances propelled me into the life of teaching.

Mrs. C taught grades 8 to 12 Foods and Clothing in Armstrong for $1620 per year. She had approximately 200 students. No preparation periods. No Professional Days. Fortunately, she had a mentor teacher (her former high school teacher from Vernon). Without her weekly meetings with this mentor, it is unlikely she would have survived her first year.

> I had no idea how to make a lesson plan. I had the course of study. I was in total confusion. I went back... I lived at home, so I went home every weekend and she [former high school teacher from Vernon] spent Saturday mornings with me and showed me how to write a lesson plan. So, she was very good at helping me on weekends. Without her help I could not flourish. And also, because I did not know what I was doing, I was up to 3:00 every morning. I got a ride from the butcher to Armstrong. I met him at the Post Office at 6:00 in the morning. But I was up 'till 3:00 doing lesson plans. And my mom stayed up until 3:00 and made me tea every half hour, just to stay with me, and she said to me at the end of the year, 'If this lifestyle is going to be too hard on you and you're not getting any sleep, I think you better consider doing something else.' But in 1949 stress wasn't a commonplace word... I mean you were stressed out, but you didn't know why... I gotta do it! But I was determined to succeed. And this how I spent my first year.
>
> The lab was in the basement of an elementary school. And when you think of a Home Ec. lab, what do you think? Stoves, fridge, washing machine? It had 3 stoves: 1 electric and 2 coal and wood stoves. From September to February, there was a recess, because this is an elementary school. From September to January, the janitor chopped the wood for me for my stove. And after February, he says, 'You've watched me chop wood, all these months, from now on it's your job.' So, every morning, when I got there at about 6:30 in the morning, I had to chop wood, to put in the coal and wood stove.
>
> There was no refrigerator. How do you run a lab without refrigeration? It was very hard. And there was no washing machine. Every day after school, I'd stay... I don't know if you know what a washboard was... It was a corrugated piece of glass on a wooden frame... and you put it into a tub, and you filled it with soapy water, and you rubbed your clothes against the

scrub-board. Every night I had to hand wash all the tea towels. Because if I didn't do it, there'd be none to use the next day. And in this teaching situation, because there were two coal or wood stoves, we ran out of kindling, the kids would put the wooden spoons in there to keep the fires going… It was the most archaic lab you could ever have in the world. I had eight treadle sewing machines in a row. There was foods on one side and clothing on the other side. The grade 8s didn't know how to treadle/propel their feet, so I had to get on my hands and knees and hand pump the treadle to make them get the rhythm of going back and forth, with the same amount of pressure, so that the machine will keep going, this way… Once you lose the pressure, the machine goes backwards and the thread breaks. So, that was a really trying year… and I don't know why I came back for more.

Anyway, I finished that year, and I came back to UBC and finished off two more years and got my BHE. At that time, you had the option of taking one year of teacher training or three years of summer school. Well, I didn't have the money… I saved a lot of money, but not enough to go for one year of teacher training, so I went to three summer schools in Victoria. And you had to take 15 units of work. For me, it was easy because I already knew what the classroom experience was like because I was immersed in it earlier. All the other people had never been in the classroom, so that was a piece of cake. But my big mistake was, had I stayed on for one more summer school, and took 15 more units of Mickey Mouse courses, I could have got a master's degree. But I said to myself after three summer schools, nah… somebody's going to say, 'hey you're not a bad person, I'll marry you.' I'll find a husband… I'll never have to teach again! So, I didn't take the 15 units, but I wish I had, because it would have put me on a different salary scale.

## 2    Reflections on Race and Ethnicity

Anyway, I graduated and then when I came to apply for a job, the head of the Home Ec. Dept. at UBC said to me, she called me in, she says 'When you send in applications for a posting, for a teaching position, your first line of your resume will say that you are of Chinese origin.' I said, "Why would I put that in my resume? That's not how you start a resume." She said, 'Because your last name is 'Joe' – J-O-E… They will think you are a First Nations, and you won't stand a chance.' So that was my first exposure to maybe there was a little racial thing to this… maybe I'm not in the right profession. Maybe, I'm obviously Chinese. I can't change that. But she said make sure on the first line you say you're of Chinese origin."

When I graduated, I said to myself, OK, I'd like to apply to Vancouver but because I'm Chinese, maybe Vancouver will only take the top 10 and I won't stand a chance. But just at that same time, one of the girls ahead of me in Home Ec., was teaching in Lumby and she said, 'I'm moving to the junior high in Vernon… there will be a vacancy, do you want to come and take my vacancy?' So, immediately I applied to the Lumby School Board and because somebody was moving on, I got into Lumby.

Again, the racial question arose… which… I guess I'm a banana… Yellow on the outside and White on the inside. I figure, I can speak the language as well as you can… Why am I different? Anyway, this incident happened the day before Spring Break. I was teaching a lesson on the different cuts… I had a picture, I drew a picture of a cow on the blackboard, and I was forming a this is a less tender cut, this is a tender cut… And just about 5 minutes before, I was facing the board, this was about 5 minutes before the bell rang, I heard this voice in the back of the room shout out: I'M NOT GOING TO TAKE ANY MORE SHIT FROM A GOD DAMN CHINAMAN! Well, the chalk fell out of my hand, by mouth dropped, my eyeballs must have hit the wall… And I turned around and I looked to see where the voice came from and it was a girl named "X" and I've remembered her name for 60 years… So, obviously, my ethnicity was discussed at home, and she was not very happy with it. Luckily, before the tears kept flowing down from my eyes, the bell rang to save me.

Anyway, when I went into the staff room, I was just crying my eyes out… and this English teacher, "Y," I remember her name, said to me… 'You know, every teacher is subject to some abuse… They look at you and they pick out the most obvious feature about you and complain about you… You say that old teacher, that FAT teacher, that short teacher, you know, whatever… You happen to be Chinese. So, she picked out the most obvious difference you had, and she embarked on it.' But she said, 'You know, it's from the mouth of a grade 9 student… Unfortunately, she just didn't have better control of what she wanted to say.' So, I cried, and I cried, and I cried… and I said to myself, Okay, my life is over. I'm always going to be Chinese. I'm always going to get this slur in a class, if the kids are unhappy with me. So, let's get out of it while you can. I had the whole 10 days to think about it. And in the 10 days, my final decision was, 'What the hell? If you can't accept this one slur from a young kid, how are you going to face the rest of your life being Chinese? How are you going to do it?' 'Are you going to run away every time some adversity arises? OR are you going to fight it?' So, I decided to fight it. And the first thing back at school, the first day back at school, the first person at my door was "X." She knocked on my door and said to me, 'Miss Joe, I'm very sorry I spoke out and said some terrible things about you before Spring Break, I want to apologize to you.' And I said to her, "X, you know, before Spring Break, you were very unhappy with me because I was Chinese. It's after Spring Break, I'm still Chinese and I'm going to be Chinese for the rest of my life... like it or not. If you want to come back to my class, you're welcome, you're welcome to come back to my class, but remember I can't change my stripes. I'm always going to be Chinese." It took me the whole 10 days to figure out this little... but it worked. The kid was alright for the rest [of the year]. But you know, this was the first year after graduation and I get this slur, and it was enough to throw me around the bend, but I guess I'm a fighter of sorts... and I let it, you know... Do you think I answered her appropriately? This was in 1952.

## 3   Reflections on Equity for Novice Teachers

When I first started at J.O. [John Oliver Secondary School], that was probably in 1955... or 56... I was teaching Foods and Clothing. We had a Dept. Head, who was a... she was a monster. If you were a new teacher, you'd only teach grades 8 and 9 forever... You never moved up. She had the top pick of the crop for herself. Now, when I became a Dept. Head at Tupper, I decided my teachers will never get stuck in grade 8 and 9. So, I said to them, OK... this year you're going to have grade 8 and 9. Next year you're going to have 9 and 10... you're going to follow your kids, because they know your idiosyncrasies and you know what they're up to and I tell you, they thanked me over and over again because they said, when we transfer out to another school, we can say we've had grade 10, 11 and 12 experience, only because you allowed that. And I only allowed that because I knew that at J.O., when your mom and I taught [Note: author's mother was a colleague of Mrs. C.], we'd teach 8s and 9s forever. No, I had the leftovers most of my life. I didn't ever... If I was ever in charge, as Dept. Head of Tupper for 7 years, I wanted them to, to expose them to as much of the curriculum as possible, only because they might not stay at Tupper forever... They might want to go elsewhere and there might be an opening of the Seniors, and if they had no experience, it's tough to get your foot in the door. Anything that I found that was awkward in my life, when I had the opportunity to change it for someone else, I changed it, because I didn't want them to go through the same hardships I did. Well, if you can call them hardships.

I think, for some reason, I was reasonably well-liked, and I was flexible unlike the J.O. Dept. Head, who only taught Foods her entire life... One year she found out she had a Clothing class... That Clothing class was in my spare period, so she said to me, Hazel, I've never taught clothing before and you like to teach Clothing, so it's yours. So, I went for half a year without a spare because I taught her class. She was that kind of a dictator. And I vowed, I'd never... If I had the opportunity, I'd never emulate her faults. It wasn't fair... Everybody... she had 2 spare periods and I had none! I was willing to take the falls because it added to my personality and what I wanted to do in the future. Not all adversity turns out to be a good luck thing, but for me it did. And then, each time I had a mat[ernity] leave, I wasn't going to go back because having a babysitter, even though it was going to be difficult, the Vancouver School Board phoned me every week, "Are you coming back? Are you coming back?" I said, "I haven't got a babysitter." "Well, find one!" Well, you know, finding one isn't [easy]... however, I did go back. Each time I took a mat leave, I didn't want to go back again... While, you know, I wanted to see what a full-time mother was going to be like... But each time I did go back. But my lucky thing was my husband was a waiter at Trader Vic's, which is down at the Bayshore Inn... And his shifts started at 10:30-2:30 every day and from five to midnight every day. So, when I left for school in the morning, at 8:00, he was home 'till 10:00. I had a babysitter come to the house and my two boys had two naps a day 'till age five... no complaints about being in the same room and facing one another and no fights. And then my husband was home at 2:30 but the kids were off at school and I'd come home at 4:00. So, because of our work schedule, it worked well. The babysitter had the kids only for lunch. When she got there, they were napping. They got up about quarter to 12... She gave them lunch at 1:00 and then she put them down for another nap until 2:30 when their dad came home. So, for me when I did find a babysitter, it worked out well.

4      Reflections on Being a Working Mother

Actually, I didn't teach 30 years. I taught 29 years and 6 months, because in 1955, I decided that... well, I knew my mother would be very unhappy with me if I didn't marry Chinese. And in Vernon there was no Chinese for me to marry, so along with two girls from high school that graduated with me... they were stenographers... we moved to Vancouver in the fall of '55... And we got an apartment at Hastings, East, and the two girls found jobs right away because they could type. And I went job hunting... and they said, "Can you type?" [I said] "No..." "Can you use Dictophone?" [and I said] "No..." "Can you do this?" [and I said] "No." "What can you do?" "What did you do?" [she replied] "I was a Home Ec. teacher." [They said] "Oh... Why are you not teaching?" "Well, I just needed a change." I couldn't find a job... [but] my two girlfriends [let me stay]... I was the chief cook and bottle washer, while they took in the money, and we stayed together. And in December of that year, there was a knock on my door... my two friends were out working... and there was a gentleman who got out of a taxi with a felt hat on and brief case... He knocked at my door... and I opened the door and he asked me if I was H. J., and I said "Yes." He said he's the Secretary Treasurer from the Nanaimo School Board. They were looking for a teacher from January to June to fill in for a mat[ernity] leave. And they understood I was a qualified Home Ec. teacher… Would I take the job? Well, I was living on the benevolence of my two friends, so I went, and I taught in Nanaimo from January to June. But at that time, I had a Chinese boyfriend in Vancouver, so I wasn't anxious to stay… and they asked me after the mat[ernity] leave if I wanted to come back. They asked me if I would stay there for another year. And when you have a romance going and its Chinese and your mother would be acceptable of it, you kind of… for those selfish reasons, I declined the offer to teach in Nanaimo. And when I left Nanaimo, I talked to an IE teacher, who was going to apply to the VSB… He was going to get out of Nanaimo. He said, 'And why don't you come with me?' I said, 'You know, R, they'll never take me in Vancouver… You know, I'm Chinese, eh? They got the pick of the world… Why would they pick a Chinese?' He says, 'You never know…' He said, 'OK, I've made an appointment for myself, and I'm making an appointment for you. You and I are going to meet at 12th and Granville and we'll walk to the School Board office and you're going to apply to Vancouver. I already made the appointment for you… you've got to go!' So, I went, and Vancouver accepted me.

## 5  Reflections on Gender

I had only girls until '82. The first boy that came was… He came to my door and said, 'Are you Mrs. C?' I said, 'Yes. Who are you?' 'I'm Freddy!" And I said, 'Oh Freddy, why are you at my door?' 'I'm in your class.' Oh, he's a grade 8… I said, 'Freddy, this is the first day of school, you've come to the wrong place. Go back down to the office and check your timetable'… 5 minutes later, Freddy was at my door with his timetable and he says, 'Look! I'm in your class!' It wasn't a mistake. It was Clothing! Sewing! He was the only boy in a class of girls… And the girls were all making blouses. And I figured, Freddy can't make the blouses. Anyway, I had to change… so, we were all making shorts. I'm going to tell you this funny story. Anyway, we were practicing the machines, stitching on paper, and different mediums at first… and the day came when we were actually put thread in the machine and we could sew… and I said, 'OK. Everybody quiet. I'm going to count 1-2-3 and then you can start. So, I went 1… 2… 3… and the machines all started… all of a sudden through the din of the machines, I hear this word, 'OH F!' The F-Word. I looked… I said… 'Freddy, you don't say those awful 4 letter words in my classroom!' He says, 'Oh shit. I'm sorry Mrs. C!' That was my Freddy story. That was my first boy in my Sewing class. 1982.

CHAPTER 2

# Ueda-sensei: Japanese Administrator (1956–1998)

Japanese teachers develop significant friendships and relationships through formal schooling. These lifelong friends include former teachers, classmates, *kôhai* (juniors) and *sempai* (seniors) as well as colleagues. Ueda-sensei is someone very well known to the author of this book. There have been many teacher-to-teacher conversations with Ueda-sensei, who has passed away since this research was conducted in 2002–2003. We begin with Ueda-sensei's colleagues, Yamada-sensei and Kojima-sensei, before turning our attention to Ueda-sensei's own narrative, for these stories of lived experiences are intertwined and embedded within strong collegial relationships and *kizuna* (bonds). This is the hallmark of Japan's exemplary teacher induction, the focus of the author's doctoral dissertation (Howe, 2005a, 2005b). The following narratives are excerpts from journal entries in fall 2002. As is the case with many of the teacher stories shared here, pseudonyms are used to protect their identities.

## 1 Yamada and Kojima Former Teachers and Colleagues

Mr. Yamada and Mr. Kojima are semi-retired and are former high school teachers of Ueda-sensei's daughter, Mayumi. At one time they worked together with Mr. Fuji, who went on to become the director of Tochigi's Education Center. Both Yamada-sensei and Fuji-sensei now work for the local *Chômin Sentâ* (community social services centre) while Kojima-sensei teaches part-time at a prestigious girls private school. All three gentlemen were 62 at the time of this study having been inducted into the profession of teaching at the same time – 1962. Each of their stories is like a different historical thread in the tapestry of Japan's teacher acculturation – providing a backdrop to the significant changes in the teaching profession since then.

I spoke with Yamada-sensei (age 62) on Wednesday for 75 minutes. He is Mayumi's old high school socials teacher. He retired four years ago and has spent his whole life in Sakura, Ueda-sensei's hometown. While this interview showed great promise, I came up empty. It was a big disappointment. The one important thing he said was that based on his experience at four different Tochigi high schools he feels the teachers are different within each school (counter to what others said and to what I have become to sense). His rationale for this is that some of the schools are highly specialized and gendered (for example a local agricultural school and all-boys school), and this changes the roles and duties of the teacher. In particular, he mentioned that it was easier teaching at an all-boys school, as there were less contentious issues around guidance and counseling. I think these views reflect his age and don't carry much weight today. The other thing I learned is how important it is to prepare your interview subjects for the nature of the questions. We spent about 15 minutes getting warmed up. I don't think Mayumi did a good enough job to brief him of the nature of our visit. In a way, this was like a pilot for the next interview with a veteran (Mayumi's old high school English teacher). How you ask questions makes a big difference in the responses you get.

The interview with Kojima-sensei (age 62, semi-retired, Mayumi's old high school English teacher – actually, his relationship with Mayumi was as the sponsor of the English club, not her classroom teacher) provided another unique perspective. We spoke in English and Japanese for over 2 hours at his place. He has a son (33) Tokyo University grad, and researcher at Columbia University for Meiji Company and a daughter (30) who is an art teacher in the next prefecture, Ibaraki. His wife sat at the next table, served us tea and spoke in Japanese but remained quiet for most of the "interview" part of our conversation, which was conducted largely in English. Both he and his wife live in a comfortable home in a rural part of Sakura about 5 minutes away. They exude a youthful appearance that betrays their years.

Kojima-sensei spoke at length about his teaching philosophy. He felt that learning alongside the students was critical to developing his teaching. However, Mr. Kojima did mention one influential *sempai* in his first year of teaching, but this was only after I asked him about *zatsudan* (informal teacher-to-teacher conversations) and if he had a mentor. Our conversation tended to focus on themes and incidents rather than a chronology of events.

Kojima-sensei has lived in Tochigi-ken all his life. He began teaching high school English almost by chance. His choices were limited to the two courses of study offered at Utsunomiya University: Education or Agriculture. While completing his application form his older brother, a Math major persuaded him to choose English rather than Math, which was his first choice as he was interested in architecture. Ultimately, he has no regrets and feels this was the best choice for him. While trained to teach elementary and junior high school, he passed the exams to teach at all three levels. The first opportunity came at Sakura High School where he spent 20 years as an English teacher.

The most interesting story told by Kojima-sensei was about his first- and second-year experience at Sakura High School in 1962. He admitted to being a "poor teacher" at first but became motivated at an early stage in his career to improve. He had an outstanding and dedicated student, whose enthusiasm acted as a catalyst for him to work extremely hard, staying up late studying English in order to be better prepared for their weekly tutorials and frequent discussions. "He had difficult questions, but he trusted me." The trust placed in Mr. Kojima's hands by this young man was immense and the bond they formed was considerable. Later, his star pupil returned to work with Mr. Kojima as a student teacher (but gave up teaching to go abroad and to work for a company). Kojima-sensei is looking forward with much anticipation to the upcoming class reunion in a couple of weeks when they have the opportunity to meet again.

Kojima-sensei also mentioned his experience coaching the Judo team. Again, he focused on what the students taught him rather than what he did. These became mutually beneficial relationships. The students' hard work motivated him in turn to be the best teacher he could be. This experience helped him to see students' growth leading to well-tempered and good character. His motto became, "You never fail to succeed if you practice very hard" (quote from a Judo master). Other parts of his teaching philosophy are exemplified by these quotes: "good teachers are trustworthy and are respected as leaders… studying with students is a great enjoyment to me… teachers learn from students." Finally, he mentioned the 44-year-old English department head and *sempai* (twice his age of 22) who taught him teaching pedagogy and passed down practical lessons.

## 2   Ueda-Sensei: Teacher, Principal and Community Leader

Ueda-sensei began his teaching career in 1956 at the age of 19 and devoted most of his life to teaching. For over 42 years he worked in the capacity of elementary and junior high school music teacher, vice-principal and principal in the rural community where he grew up. Even after retiring, he worked for the school board as a counselor and mentor. In retirement, he spent much of his time working in his garden, volunteering in the community and playing music. He even tutored harmonica! Like many Japanese men of his generation, he has difficulty accepting retirement… or perhaps he doesn't know how to relax. He seems to make work for himself. For example, he will find things to go and photocopy like music scores or newspaper clippings that his wife claims just end up in the trash! His other eccentric behaviour that drives family members crazy is that he can't seem to throw out anything! There is an entire room filed with old files and other relics characteristic of a teacher. Every room must have a pair of scissors, a highlighter, a pen, a pencil and a glue-stick.

Ueda-sensei says that his first years of teaching were challenging. He recalled how when he was a young teacher in Tochigi, they had to take turns performing the *shukuchoku* duty – staying overnight in the school in order to protect the school property (originally the purpose was to safeguard the picture of the Emperor). Men had to take on this responsibility from Monday to Saturday while women were obliged to help on Sunday. Colleagues often dropped by to keep those on duty company. This was a great opportunity for *zatsudan* and informal professional development. However, the Japan Teachers' Union became a lot stronger (although to this day, the Union is weaker in Tochigi and other conservative prefectures compared to Tokyo and other urban areas) and so this practice was abolished in most schools at all levels in 1973. While this extra-curricular duty was considered a burden, Ueda-sensei and others considered it a sort of self-directed professional development and an opportunity to bond with colleagues. Nevertheless, Japanese teachers still have many duties thrust upon them outside the realm of 'teaching' in the Western sense of the word.

Ueda-sensei used to ride a motor scooter to school. He spent long hours at school six or seven days a week. He would leave at dawn and return home late at night after the children had eaten their supper and were ready for bed. Teachers were highly regarded then (and now) but not well paid. It wasn't until the early 1970's they received a substantial increase in pay. Ueda-sensei indicated that despite the long hours and broader roles of teachers, they were more relaxed back then. Club activities were fun. Games were friendly encounters with opportunities to meet with colleagues from other schools rather than the daily drill and practice in preparation for the fierce competitions of today. Teachers from different schools had more time to get together informally in order to share experiences. Moreover, the kinds of people drawn to teaching were more eclectic. Today's teachers are all of one mold – high achievers, academically inclined but more egocentric and introverted.

Everyone in this small rural town of less than 20,000 seems to know Ueda-sensei. In talking to people at the local kindergarten and public schools, many teachers knew him. Also, he seems to know nearly everyone else in town. Ueda-sensei seems to be preoccupied with what everyone else thinks about him and his family. What's more, he has a way of getting his nose into everyone else's business. While Ueda-sensei cares deeply for honouring tradition and respecting others he does things that fly in the face of all his "do the right thing" attitude and ethical *sensei* mentality. Many of the following examples are characteristic of Japanese traditional practices that are still commonplace. It must be noted that these thoughts and insights reflect the Western mentality and thinking of the author and must be understood in that context.

Ueda-sensei got a phone call Saturday from Mayumi's cousin asking her to help him with his *natsu-yasumi shukudai* (homework to be completed over the summer vacation). What he really wanted was for her to do it for him! Of course, like all students, this boy left his English essay until the last minute and when Mayumi asked him to fax his work in progress, there were only a few incoherent phrases patched together by blank spaces. I was surprised that rather than chastising them, Ueda-sensei insisted that the paragraph be written by Mayumi and then proofread by me! Then it had to be copied out in BLOCK LETTERS and faxed to these relatives immediately because it was due the next day. Now, for this to happen would not be unusual in some situations (like a farming family that doesn't care about schooling) but for a retired principal bent on taking traditional proper customs excruciatingly to the extreme – that is surprising! Why isn't doing your nephew's homework the "wrong" thing to do? If this is condoned here, is it widespread? Do students even consider this cheating? Perhaps, it isn't considered "wrong" because it doesn't count for marks.

Is it right for an adult to help a child with his homework? How about asking a nearly native English speaker to write an English paragraph? Mayumi was asked by both her niece and nephew to do their homework! It is one thing to ask for help, but in this case, Mayumi was asked to write the paragraph from scratch! This amounted to plagiarism! I asked if this was considered ethically and morally acceptable in Japan? Ueda-sensei's response was that while it is 'wrong' it is more important to maintain good relations with family than to take the moral high ground. Also, he indicated that homework was not the same as a test. Students consider homework as a duty that must be done but it doesn't 'count' for marks. Therefore, doing someone else's homework is not on the same level as writing a test for them, which is definitely considered a serious kind of cheating. What is the purpose of homework, if students can get all sorts of help with it... and if it doesn't count anyways, why do it at all? Well, there is a sense of not wanting to disappoint the teacher more so than the parents. Students respect their teachers and will go to great lengths to (on the surface) try to do their homework, to honour their wishes and to not disappoint them.

Japanese principals wield a great deal more power than their Western counterparts. This is not a problem, provided they are reasonable, fair and collegial. However, that is not always the case. Ueda-sensei contacted the principal of a local elementary school, where the author was conducting research. Ueda-sensei insisted on calling this principal to inform him with details of plans to "interview" two new teachers. He felt we needed the principal's permission to visit the school and talk with these teachers. It is their duty to record any visits in a book (including the names of the visitors and the nature of their visit). Ueda-sensei felt the researcher should have prepared a more detailed and comprehensive "questionnaire" in advance, faxed it to these teachers and their principal for their approval and convenience and then conducted a structured interview. It is likely Ueda-sensei feared teachers will paint a different picture of their Principal and it would make Ueda-sensei look bad.

According to Ueda-sensei this principal is difficult to deal with and yet according to another teacher-participant, he is easy-going! The teachers were instructed not to share anything beyond what is in "the book on new teachers" (of course as the questions involve opinions this is impossible). This is analogous to a union boss telling teachers not to speak to the press during a strike about the nature of the struggle, for fear that what is reported won't reflect the "official union stance" or a politician being directed by the Prime Minister to tow the party-line. This does not bode well for a social democratic nation and egalitarian workplace. Secondly, the Principal suggested that it was dangerous to conduct these interviews and publish research abroad–disseminating potential misinformation to the world. He questioned the wisdom of interviewing his teachers in fear that the researcher would base all observations, interpretations and analysis on the opinions of just two teachers under his direct supervision and authority. The principal (and likely Ueda-sensei) is concerned with his reputation. If the teachers are overly critical, it will reflect poorly on his leadership (or lack of). Clearly there is a power imbalance in the principal-teacher relationship.

These new teachers are now afraid to speak their minds for fear of the repercussions (first-year teachers are on probation). Principals in Japan expect to be informed of anything that involves teachers under their supervision. So, if a researcher were to meet with teachers outside school in their free time, they would need the permission of their principal!

Like their Western counterparts, new teachers in Japan tend to get all the tasks no one cares for. How else could you explain that both new teachers at this elementary school have been assigned the duty of taking care of the school during *o-bon*? This is the most important Japanese family holiday of the year, when businesses shut down, the roads fill with people returning home, when relatives come from all over to pay respects to their ancestors. Of course, it is a holiday for all teachers, (who would voluntarily work during a national holiday) yet all day on August 15th and 16th the new teachers have been ordered to be on duty–what on earth for? Is this a national tradition? I am told they will carry out mundane chores like watering plants and answering the phones! I have to infer that the new teachers were chosen for these days specifically because they are neophytes. Nevertheless, the likelihood of anyone phoning or visiting is next to nil. It is interesting to note that in the West, it is the principal or vice principal who comes to school during the summer vacation to take care of administrative duties rather than teachers.

CHAPTER 3

# Clare: Home Economics Secondary & Post-Secondary Teacher (1958–1995)

Clare was born and raised in Enderby, BC. She had an older sister that went into teaching, a younger sister that went to secretarial school, and a younger brother who became a pharmacist. Maybe if she had been born a few decades later, Clare would have pursued a career in pharmacy too, but in the mid-20th century, girls were rarely encouraged to go beyond high school, let alone to study sciences. Nevertheless, Clare's mother encouraged her to continue her studies and to be a strong young woman. Clare remembers her junior high school math teacher fondly and loved mathematics. Clare entered teaching as there were few post-secondary choices for girls back then other than teaching or nursing. Her high school principal recommended Clare study home economics at the University of British Columbia (UBC). Clare graduated with a Bachelor of Home Economics in 1957 and then did an additional year and one summer session of teacher education to obtain her Permanent Teaching Certificate. Clare recalls being pulled out of a teacher education class in her final months at UBC by a recruiter from the BC interior, who offered her a job on the spot. In those days, there were no job fairs. Instead, school board representatives from various school districts across the province came to UBC and pulled students out of classes to interview them.

## 1   Junior High School Teaching

Clare's first teaching job was at Princess Margaret Elementary and Junior High School in Penticton, BC. It was a challenging job for a beginning teacher in that it was a new school with nothing set up yet. Home economics was scheduled in one large room where both the foods and sewing courses were to be taught. As the only home economics teacher, she had to set up the classroom for both foods and sewing classes. This was a huge task as there were boxes of equipment that had to be organized into six separate workstations. Her workload consisted of preparing for and teaching all grade 7, 8, 9, food and clothing courses, a grade 8 math course (for which she had no background), supervising and accounting for a home room class of 35 students in addition to doing corridor and yard supervision before and after school. Teaching math was relatively easy, as a textbook was supplied and followed, which simplified lesson planning and preparation. In all her years of teaching, Clare only had one minor discipline problem. It occurred in the Math class during her first year of teaching. Several boys would not give Clare their full attention. Clare stopped speaking for a long minute, then said "Do you realize I am being paid to teach you some math and you obviously are not interested. You are wasting my time, so I am leaving." Frustrated, she went to the staff room. It was not long before there was a knock on the door. One of the troublemakers, with his head down said, "Sorry Miss D., I have come for the whole class – we are ready to learn." And learn they did!

With the home economics courses, a skeleton curriculum was provided and from there the teacher had to prepare lessons to facilitate the required learning. The foods course was the most time consuming, in that food had to be ordered, purchased, broken down into sizeable amounts, and distributed to the various units. Demonstrations were required prior to the students doing labs, so setups had to be ready in order to carry this out. Each unit had to be checked out at the end of each lab to make sure it was clean, garbage removed to the main garbage container, and all the equipment in the proper place for the next class to use. Clare also had laundry to contend with as well as keeping all areas of the room clean and in good working order. The principal hinted it would be nice if the *Home Ec Girls* occasionally supplied the staff with cookies. While some colleagues bent to the principal's requests, Clare told him she didn't see it noted in the prescribed curriculum... Enough is enough!

The clothing class was easier, as a project was chosen, the students brought what they needed to execute it, and then the lab progressed over time. Teaching involved demonstrations, display samples, guiding and supervising each student's work, and keeping the machines and equipment in good working order. When it came to sewing, Clare learned a lot alongside her students as she had little sewing experience beyond her UBC coursework. Her younger sister who had taken home economics in high school had to teach Clare thimble drill (this helps one use a thimble when hand sewing), which in turn she taught to her students. To start with she let the grade 9 students pick any pattern to work on as long as it included certain details. Grade 7 and 8 students did not have this opportunity as they were beginners.

Clare's homeroom class of grade 9 students was held in her home economics lab. They were a great group, and often on Fridays at the end of day after study hour they would volunteer to help Clare fold the laundry and do other tasks. Sometimes to thank students, Clare would surprise them with a demonstration of something that was easy to make. As well, she always had samples for them to try. They loved this, and often on Monday mornings, many of the boys would arrive with what they had made over the weekend, for her to evaluate.

They were always very productive, working on homework, in this study hour in hopes there might be a surprise cooking demonstration and treats to follow.

The junior high section of the school often had social events that the staff had to attend. Clare always enjoyed participating in these. One event was a skating party at the local arena. The *big boys* thought it would be fun to have Miss D. at the end of a long crack the whip line. They were very disappointed however, when Clare would never fall down or go flying off the line.

Teaching wasn't all fun and games, however. Newly appointed teachers were in essence on probation until they received satisfactory evaluations. Teaching evaluations were a bit nerve racking. The inspector from Victoria would arrive and spend the entire day. Generally, reports were always good, but, with no constructive criticism, these assessments were of little value. Clare was disappointed not to receive any meaningful feedback as there is always room to improve and better ways of doing things. Clare enjoyed teaching in Penticton for two years, but because it was a small town, she accepted a position in Vancouver, BC.

Clare's next job was at John Oliver Secondary School in Vancouver. From 1960-1962, Clare taught junior foods and sewing classes at John Oliver. Given she had two years teaching experience under her belt it was an easier time but still a heavy load. She had two separate labs: a foods lab on the first floor and a sewing lab on the third floor, so she had to travel up and down several times a day. Clare remembers teaching a sewing class to a challenged special needs group of 12 girls.

> They were such an affectionate group… and expressed such worry on Fridays that I would not return on Monday. They really kept me on my toes as I discovered it had to be one on one teaching… When it came to using the sewing machine – they were the engine (power), and I would help them steer.

This was highly individualized teaching. In a sense, perhaps this was similar to our Individualized Education Plans (IEP) for our special education students. But now teachers have Educational Assistants (EAs) and other supports in place. Clare said she did not know how to use a sewing machine, nor had she sewn a garment before she entered UBC. She felt in the long run that perhaps this lack of experience helped her to both teach and relate to these challenged students. These students were very dear to Clare and in the end both she and they were very happy and proud in that they had produced a simple top and skirt. They even decided to invite their parents and friends to school one lunch hour so they could model their outfits runway style.

Students and their parents were always on the minds of teachers. On one occasion, Clare and a colleague decided to go to the Fraser Arms for a drink after work. But when they realized the local pub was filled with parents of students, they beat a hasty retreat and made other plans. You see, while it might not seem an indiscretion today, in the 1960s, teachers, in particular women teachers, were held to high moral standards. Rather than be seen going to the local pub for a beer after work on a Friday, Clare and a female colleague would sometimes go to The White Spot drive-in restaurant for a coffee – a safe alternative.

## 2        Post-Secondary Teaching

In 1962, at the age of 27, Clare was asked by the head of the Home Economics Department to teach the beginning foods course at UBC as well as being the Home Management House Advisor. Clare accepted this very prestigious opportunity for professional growth... And growth it was, as she had no advanced foods degree. So happily, she learned and happily she taught... She was encouraged if not almost threatened to get a master's degree, but she declined, for she never intended to stay at UBC. Her salary and benefits were less than in the K-12 public school system. To enrich herself she would take summer courses at other universities, plus spend a lot of time in their libraries. Clare attended Kansas State, Nevada State, UCLA Davis Campus, and Oregon State.

During her time at UBC, Clare was responsible for the introductory foods course which included 3 hours of lecture and many 3-hour lab sections. The lab section prep was a great deal of work. First decisions had to be made as to what was to be done and by whom. Market orders for food and equipment not housed in the lab had to be turned in one week in advance. The lab setup for the week involved distribution of required food and extra equipment in each unit along with individual instruction cards pertaining to the specific assignment involved. The preparation and placement of visual displays for the week often involved food preparation and had to be set up. This was also time consuming, but both Clare and her students found them very interesting and enriching. During each lab, demonstrations were often done, and this required separate organized food and equipment setups to carry this out. Extra lab handouts had to be put together for distribution and use during the lab. The set up for the week was always done by Clare on Sundays. There was not enough time for this on Mondays as she had an 8:30 am lecture and her first lab section started at 2:30 pm.

Help involved a pantry technician who would obtain the food for all the labs, do the laundry and cleaning. Class sizes varied from about 60 to 150 students which were broken down into four to eight lab sections. To help with the labs, Clare had lab assistants whose responsibility was to teach and grade one or more of the lab sections. These lab assistants were often former students, who were married and wanted part time work. They were a great help and often offered constructive ideas. After fifteen years of teaching the School moved to a new building. Clare faced many challenges with the new lab as the space was much smaller. During her first lab set up of the year she actually cried "How can I make this work?" Because of the layout, much more organization was involved, which meant more time. Because the lab technician and lab assistants were part time, Clare was often left to clean the labs at the end of the term. There simply wasn't enough in the budget to hire help.

The lecture part of the foods course had to be taught in another building as there was not a large enough room in the old building. In her first years, Clare taught in the old M huts, relics from WWII barracks, still on campus. Later she was able to teach in more sophisticated lecture halls. Fortunately, when the new building came to be Clare had the coveted MWF 8:30 am slot in the large lecture room... No more having to travel outside especially in bad weather!

Back then, Clare's teaching tools were simply chalk and board with very few handouts. It was a great improvement when overhead projectors arrived on the scene plus photo-coping, which meant lecture outlines could be distributed, which helped, especially given the fact the food chemistry part of the course was expanding, as the focus was on the "why" and not just the "how."

In the first several years of her teaching, Clare was Home Management House Adviser which involved living in a house on the UBC campus, in a remote location, amongst the trees, with four separate suites (three were for students and one unit was for the instructor). Home economics students in their fourth year were required to spend two weeks living in this home as part of their coursework. Clare was responsible for maintaining the house for 12 months of the year. In the summer the suites were rented out and Clare lived elsewhere. Many times, the renters left a mess, and it was Clare's job to clean up and ready the home for another school year. The suites varied in size and luxury and had different budgets for foods. Clare supervised and evaluated how successful students were in managing one of the three different suite experiences. The first night in the house involved having all 8 students in the instructor's suite where an overview of the course was provided. The first time around this was a bit of a choking disaster as Clare thought it might be nice to light the wood fireplace... but unfortunately, she did not know it was necessary to open the damper and so smoke filled the home! As years passed, the Home Management House course was dropped, and Clare's Introductory Foods course evolved to more and more food science. As well, she taught a consumer foods course and an experimental lab course for a short time. But Clare was happy this was only for a while as it was a great deal of extra work.

Clare recalled a number of memorable students... There was girl for example who had worked for Bonnie Stern, a famous Toronto celebrity chef, who ran a cooking school. This student was taking a course with Clare and she was in Clare's lab section too. Interestingly, this girl compared Clare to the famous Bonnie Stern and Ms. Stern's culinary knowledge. Clare responded by saying, "Good! You have been so enriched with Ms. Stern's knowledge. So, you should be able to get a very good mark in this class!" Clare used to say to students, "Ask me anything. Don't expect me to have the answer. Let's all see if we can find the answer." Clare remembered another star pupil who distinguished herself. In Clare's experimental foods course this student was working on a collaborative project with a fish processing company. The project's objective was to produce a sauce to be included in canned herring. This clever girl produced a tomato sauce that was so tasty the company decided to use it in all their canned herring sold in retail. This was very satisfying for Clare to know that her students were able to find successful careers as teachers, dieticians or even as entrepreneurs.

While working at UBC, Clare had several episodes of fires to deal with. In Home Management House each group of girls in the main suite had to put on one formal dinner to which they each invited a guest and of course Clare was there as she always ate the evening meal with them. Clare could also invite a guest, so there were usually ten to prepare for. One group decided to have a dramatic entrée – *flaming* beef shish-kabobs. Flaming they were, to the point the flames could not be put out and the entire dinner party ended up outside. What caused the flames to burn so violently? Apparently, the girls had doused the kabobs with 100% alcohol... No meat course that night!

The second incident occurred in her foods lab in the old building. On a Friday evening, while at home, Clare received a phone call from the head of the department saying her lab was on fire and not to come out to UBC, as there was little that could be done that night. She was very worried that the instructor teaching the Friday lab had not checked to see everything was off before she left. Clare came out to examine the damage the next day and she walked into a completely black hole from top to bottom. Everything was covered with soot. Thankfully, she was not responsible. Some chemicals used by the Nutrition people, which were held in a small room off the lab had ignited. A new lab had to be set up for Monday. What to do? Fortunately, the other foods lab was not being used, so on Sunday Clare *had fun* setting it up for the week and both she and the students had to adapt to this new environment which was not nearly as compatible space wise. The third fire incident occurred in her lab in the new building. Clare had designed a unique demonstration table with overhead mirror and a section of the top surface that could be removed to expose four electric elements should she need to heat something. One day after Clare had finished the morning lab section, while she was sitting in the adjoining technician's area having lunch with the tech, they thought they heard a crackling sound. When it continued, they went to investigate. To their horror they discovered a brown round mark on the top of the demo table covering the elements. Smoke was exiting from the cracks. Somehow the elements were on under the replaced top. Drama again! UBC fireman arrived on the scene and handled the situation. Fortunately, the labs were able to continue to the end of term even though the table surface was scared and the elements non-functional. The table was repaired, and a safety mechanism was added... That should have been done in the first place.

As Clare did not do research, she was given the job of course scheduling for the department. It was a real puzzle to put together a timetable with no clashes for all the Home Economics, Dietetics, Nutrition, Clothing, Design, Management and Family Science courses and as well have them mesh with all the Arts, Science and Agriculture courses the students took. Course scheduling also involved finding and assigning classroom space for each of the courses. Clare often joked, "She *published* once a year – the departments timetable!" Registration usually ran smoothly, except for one incident in her early years of being in charge. At that time, she was asked to create a group of set timetables for the first-year students. These included all their required arts and science courses, so come registration week they were already placed into certain course sections. During registration week, the individual in charge of scheduling for the English department phoned to tell Clare she had created an English 100 section for Home Economics students that did not exist! This was devastating, as it meant nothing in the schedule would work if they had to use another section of English 100. To her relief, the dear English department person said he could use another section for other students and so that section came into existence. No more problem.

As well, Clare was in charge of setting up and running registration week, which involved course cards before registration went online in the mid-to-late 1980s. Once registration was computerized, she controlled the registration online. To facilitate this, Clare was given Dean's access to courses and student records. One summer they even set up Clare's UBC computer at her home to control registration which took place over the summer. This was because Clare had fallen and broken her hip one Sunday going in to set up the last lab of the year. Clare managed to make her way to a desk phone. She called her niece, who was living on campus, to come and help her. Clare had to slide on her bottom down a long hall to let her niece in. Her niece took her to UBC hospital. Clare really should have phoned 911. As it was the last week of classes, lectures and labs were cancelled. Many students came to visit Clare in hospital to cheer her up.

Clare also became Senior Adviser for both the Home Economics and Dietetics programs. With this came the extra responsibility of maintaining all students' records, as well as checking to see all their course requirements were met for graduation. With her lab contacts, her advising and her open-door policy, she got to know many of her students very well and easily developed rapport. She even gave them her home phone number if they needed help or had a specific question, they thought she could answer. It was never abused. Clare received a prestigious teaching award in 1995 at fall convocation. She was very well liked by most of her students. In a sense, they were like family to her. In 1990 Clare was one of 75 UBC faculty and staff from all areas to receive a 75th anniversary service medal for her efforts beyond the call of duty. Clare retired from UBC in 1997, after 35 years of service.

CHAPTER 4

# Norma: K-16 Teacher (1967–2017)

1        From Rural Alberta to Urban British Columbia

Norma has taught from kindergarten through post-secondary. Her career spans five decades (from 1967–2007 K-12 in Alberta and BC and then at Thompson Rivers University from 2007–2017).

Norma was born and raised in rural Alberta. She grew up in a small town, east of Edmonton, near the Saskatchewan border. Everyone knew one another. Life was simple. Norma's father and her grandfather were both farmers. Norma's grandmother was a teacher. Norma and most of her neighbours lived on farms. The long winters were cold with lots of snow! Getting to school could pose a serious challenge. Students were often not able to get to school until the snowplow came through. While her older siblings rode a horse to school and attended a one-roomed school with multi-graded classes, by the time Norma started school she was bused to a larger modern school with one or two classes per grade, as was typical for Alberta schools then. In any case, even though it was a larger school with many students, there were no students, teachers or staff of colour. But there was a large population of Ukrainian students as 1955 was a time when many Ukrainian immigrants came to Alberta to farm. The one major exception was a teacher from Africa. In those days, the population was expanding and there was a shortage of teachers, so teachers had to be recruited from all over. First Nations students went to the local residential day school, but Norma and others were unaware of this situation. However, some Indigenous students attended Norma's school as they lived off the reserve and may have had a non-Indigenous father. Clearly, race and diversity were not part of rural Alberta schooling in the 1950s and 1960s.

In the late sixties when Norma started teaching in Red Deer, the only immigrant Norma remembers from her early teaching days was one boy from Scotland. There were no children of colour. Nevertheless, there was an industrial residential school not far from Red Deer. Some shocking and disturbing facts about this school and other residential schools across Canada have recently come to light as human remains have been found in nearby fields and by the river.

Norma always wanted to be a teacher, but it was not her first choice. It was rather a practical choice, as girls did not have many career choices other than teacher or nurse in the 1960s. Norma could not recall any girls studying to become a lawyer, doctor or engineer. It was rare for a girl to enter those professions.

> Well, I always wanted to be a teacher when I was young going through school. In grade 12 I started thinking about it. I had two older sisters that were teachers, and one was teaching me at the time. I thought – I don't want to be a teacher. So, I applied to get into physiotherapy, but I didn't get in. I was accepted at the University of Alberta, but not in physiotherapy. So, I still could go register. I needed to make a choice: what am I going to register in today that I can get in? I registered in the arts. I went back to my residence and thought, do I really want to do that? No. So, the next day I went back, and I went into education. I look back on it and realize education was something I wanted to do. I didn't actually finish my degree till after I was married and had family when I finished my BEd.

Norma attended the University of Alberta for two years and was granted a provisional teaching certificate in 1967. In those days, you could start teaching with just two years of post-secondary. Her education included several brief practica with observations and some teaching. The longest practicum in her second year was six weeks. Norma indicated that she felt ill-prepared for the challenges faced in her first year of teaching. In particular, as an elementary teacher, she had to teach all subjects from science to physical education.

As was typically done by teachers then, the focus was on the three Rs: reading, writing and arithmetic. Norma taught from readers and workbooks. She had three reading groups. The lowest group was always together. Teachers used the Gestetner machine, producing those purple worksheets that smelled like a distillery.

> Because when you wanted to copy you used that thing. You turned the alcohol upside down and hoped that it didn't spill and that it went in the way it was supposed to and you ran off these sheets and then you brought the sheets back to the classroom. And if they were newly duplicated the kids all sniffed them because they smelt so good. Seriously. It was quite funny. You had to make sure you got your copying done well before class or else you had kids sniffing alcohol.

There weren't any inclusive lesson plans, or any accommodations made for exceptionality or special needs students. Students sat in rows and were placed in one of the three groups based on their assessed reading levels.

> It was certainly, you know, I almost say baptism by fire because there wasn't a lot of good prep then for beginning teachers. And you taught the basic arithmetic, reading, writing and spelling, all different subjects, science and socials which were out of textbooks. There wasn't a lot of hands-on for science, for sure. I'm not sure if there was even any kind of equipment in that little school in Red Deer.

Norma's teaching career spans five decades from kindergarten through post-secondary. She started teaching in 1967 in Red Deer Alberta. It was Canada's Centennial year. Norma was asked to teach grade 4 at a new elementary school. As the school was still under construction when it opened in September, she had to share a space with another grade 4 teacher, who was a seasoned veteran. The "mud room" in the basement had a curtain to divide each classroom but the sounds from each class easily penetrated this portable barrier. This "mud room" as Norma called it, is much like a multi-purpose room in today's schools but without any frills. It was simply a space where rows of desks could be easily set up and a class could be conducted from outside the cold. Presumably all a teacher needed in those days was a chalkboard, textbooks and obedient students. Norma felt the other veteran teacher must have been distracted by Norma's loud teaching voice, but this arrangement did not present any serious problems for her students. Norma couldn't recall where the students put their boots, jackets, and knapsacks though, as there was no cloakroom like most classes. Perhaps these things were simply placed on the floor at the back of the room. Norma called her first year of teaching a "baptism by fire" as it was very challenging, but it was also a good learning experience.

## 2    Religion in Schools

In the late 1960s, when Norma started teaching, The Lord's Prayer and reading of scriptures from the Bible were an integral part of daily routines. This practice stems from the fact that public schools and the School Act of 1905 had Christian teachings mandated. In 1967, there was a Christian textbook prescribed in the Alberta curriculum. Teachers were expected to read a specific scripture to students each day. What you were to read was clearly set out by authorities but there was no room for discussion, interpretation or critical analysis. With the advent of sweeping changes in schooling across Canada, the reading of scriptures was stopped a few years after Norma started teaching but The Lord's Prayer was something she continued to do with students. While

The Lord's Prayer and other Christian artifacts still remain in some Canadian schools, this changed in the 1970s as religion was taken out of public schooling in most Canadian provinces. Interestingly, religion in Alberta's public schools recently made headlines in the news as some parents are questioning if it is appropriate to be reciting The Lord's Prayer. It remains a controversial topic, but Alberta is not known as a "Bible belt" and in fact many Albertans claim not to practice any religion at all.

## 3 Special Visits from VIPs: Superintendent and Governor General

All new teachers were on probation until they had received two visits from the Superintendent. Norma noted that these visits were usually unannounced and random. "There was never any warning… He was just there." Norma recalled one such visit where she was giving a spelling test. It did not seem like the best time for an administrator to observe her teaching! The Superintendent would visit, observe a class and then write up a report. If you received two satisfactory reports, then you were taken off probation and granted a teaching licence. But he was not the only VIP to visit Red Deer in that year.

In 1967, Roland Michener, the Governor General of Canada was trying to visit as many schools as possible as part of the Canadian Centennial celebrations. It just happened that Roland Michener's family had a farm not far from Red Deer. So, Norma's school district was conveniently selected as one of the Governor General's designated stops. All the grade 6 students had the opportunity to go listen to his speech at the local arena. It was Roland Michener's tradition to thank everyone for attending and to announce to his audiences that "You all have Monday off school!" This meant that all classes in Red Deer were cancelled on the following Monday. When Roland Michener gave an order, teachers and others obeyed! Can you imagine that happening today?

## 4 Discipline

Classroom management is an important part of teaching. But things have changed a great deal since Norma's early teaching days.

> It was a grade 1 to 6 school. And it was… yes, it was interesting. I mean, in those days you still [had corporal punishment]… the strap was still used by the principal, occasionally. Well, you know, it was a different era. You never saw parents in the classroom helping out. Discipline was totally

different, of course, then. I mean, I remember putting kids in a corner. I wouldn't do that now for all the tea in China. I learned that's not how we get kids to [behave]. We don't need to use the word "discipline" as far as I'm concerned. Whereas when I started teaching, we learned how to do discipline. How are we going to punish them? Whereas now we look at things differently when children are not doing what is expected of them.

## 5 Assessment

Assessment is another thing that has really changed since Norma started teaching.

> It was all tests, as you assessed your children with marking and tests, and there was no kind of holistic marking. Like, the idea of using criteria, I don't think I ever used criteria until I got into criteria marking after we moved to BC in 1988. In the early 1990s, I began criteria marking. Before that when you marked something, you gave them a mark and then you added the marks up and that's what they got on their report card. All handwritten. And that was assessment. Or tests, like, even the times when I taught high school in the 1970s, it was all tests with some writing. They'd write it for you, and you'd mark, but, you know, it was sort of like look at it, okay… that's a four out of ten. Or that's a six out of ten – There wasn't really any criteria. The way now, I mean, even in my university teaching I used criteria for my marking, and I used it in my last years of teaching before I retired. But, assessment – well, yet I say that and yet I know that some places, from what I hear, the students talk about sometimes some assessment hasn't come a long ways. There's still a right and a wrong and, I mean, you used to put the names up of the people that got the best marks. Poor kids that were always at the bottom of the sheet. And I did that too. Now I just shudder when I think about it. Doing that kind of thing. So, the whole idea about criteria, looking at criteria and marking is probably the hugest change that I know, that I see.

CHAPTER 5

# Terry: Nova Scotia/NWT/BC (1971–)

Terry grew up in Halifax and started his long teaching career there at an inner-city Halifax school. It was 1971. Like many teachers, he got into teaching rather accidentally. As a young man, in his early twenties, he fell into teaching. Terry soon discovered that he really loved teaching and it became his lifelong passion.

> I'd just graduated and was looking to go to law school… but needed some money. They were offering free tuition to any student who took a Bachelor of Education (BEd) program and a guaranteed job at the end of it. So, I thought, well, I don't have to pay tuition. I can take get a BEd and I can go and do some Teacher on Call (TOC) work while I'm working my way through school.

Terry found that he really liked teaching. He liked working with kids. He liked being in classrooms. So, even though Terry was on a list to be admitted to law school, he never pursued it. Terry continued to work in education and the more he worked in it, the more he liked it.

It is remarkable to think that Terry enjoyed teaching, despite the fact he started his teaching at an impoverished inner-city school with very challenging students. In Terry's first year of teaching, he taught grade 6 at an inner-city school, not far from where he grew up. It is one of Halifax's poorest communities, and one of the most violent crime areas in the Maritimes. This part of Halifax had a lot of public housing. Terry's students were of low socioeconomic status and really disadvantaged. In fact, at one time in the 1970s, this area had one of the highest murder rates in Canada. So, it was in a disadvantaged inner-city school, where Terry started teaching, a career that has spanned five decades. Terry has taught in several very different parts of Canada (Nova Scotia, Northwest Territories and BC). Moreover, Terry's contributions have ranged from classroom teacher, to administrator and superintendent. To honour his voice and extensive experience, the following transcript is offered verbatim from our *teacher-to-teacher conversation* in 2016, after Terry had retired from his job as superintendent. For more than a decade, Terry has worked as a sessional faculty member, teaching a variety of graduate courses in leadership, including legal issues. In 2020, Terry was called back to the school district as acting superintendent during the COVID-19 pandemic. He has been kept very busy with this important and challenging work!

## 1 Changes in Curriculum, Teaching and Learning and Special Education

How has curriculum, teaching and learning changed over the last 40 years? That is a very interesting question. I look back on my first year of teaching… I think I had 38 students. There weren't any special needs students in my class. There weren't any special needs classrooms. I think we had the first one, which my mother actually was a leader in getting because I had a brother with Downs Syndrome… And of course, [those] children were not allowed in the public education system. So back in the mid 50's and early 60's, she led the charge to get the first special needs classroom in the Halifax public system. So, we still didn't have a lot when I started in 1971. We had some speech pathologists in the system but that was about it.

[It was a] standardized curriculum – you taught everything. You taught a set curriculum and were monitored very closely by the principal to ensure that you were on such-and-such a page of the math book on such-and-such a day. And your plan books were examined on a regular basis to see how you were progressing through the curriculum. Corporal punishment was a regime, and we were issued with a box of chalk and a strap, or we were directed to buy a strap. You could go to the teachers supply stores in Halifax and you could buy one [and even] get your choice of an orange one or purple one or black one. Something that would go with the décor in your classroom if you like. I never bought one. I never had one. But it was very difficult because you were often directed by the principal to administer corporal punishment which I found to be very, very difficult. And luckily a few years later I think most school boards in Canada outlawed it although it was still permitted. And it is still permitted to some degree under the Charter. But it was hard. With respect to that, that was a system I grew up in. And so, looking at it from the other end, especially in a community where I lived and where children were very disadvantaged it was difficult. So that was the management skills that you were expected to have.

There wasn't any support. You didn't see special needs children. The group was fairly homogeneous as far as their abilities were concerned, but there wasn't any real differentiation of instruction. And there wasn't any real attempt, I think, to try and meet the needs of students, although I would, and younger teachers that were starting with me, would help students after school. We had 16 teachers on staff, 14 of us were first-year teachers, by the way. And we couldn't get teachers fast enough across the country. It was a time of expanding systems. I think in 1967 or 1968 British Columbia opened a new school for every day school was in session during that year. So, the system was exploding. We couldn't keep pace. We couldn't keep up with facilities. We couldn't hire enough teachers. It was a time where you could get a job anywhere in Canada that you really wanted. So, we had 14 first-year teachers. We had one teacher with three years' experience, and I think one with five years' experience and then a new principal. And that was the staff. So that was a sense of where we were.

We decided that year that we would do a Christmas concert because the school hadn't had a Christmas concert for a very long time. So, we each decided, you know, something that we would do, and we put the Christmas concert on. But the Christmas concert started at 7:00 and it was still going at 11:00 that night. Because we didn't [plan well] and the parents stayed, but we had some homeless people that drifted in. And they were laying down in the aisles and sleeping while the Christmas concert progressed. So, it was a learning experience for us… it was the longest Christmas concert I ever attended or ever put on! But it was basically because so many of us were just so inexperienced. And even the teachers with three and four years of experience had never done it before. So that was just one example of this critical mass of new teachers and new energy that came into the system. We really wanted to work hard to meet the needs of the children. But it was a learning experience for all of us. We did have a meeting with the superintendent. The superintendent called all new teachers to a meeting with him, and I remember the meeting very distinctly. Because he said, basically, this is the way it's going to be, and I can't remember him describing the way it was going to be, and if you don't like it, then go get a job somewhere else. So, that's when I applied to go to Yellowknife after that meeting.

You just had to have what they called two years of normal college. So, you went to grade 12 and then you took two years at a normal college and then they gave you a licence to teach. For some people it was even less than that. But we have to remember that school districts were faced with a problem of not having enough teachers for start-up in September. With this huge demand, these large families (I came from a family of seven and next door to us had 12 and another family down the street had 17). People had huge families, and there was this tremendous pressure. The school districts were sending out recruiting teams all over the world and you couldn't get teachers. So, normal colleges were quite common. As a matter of fact, Lyndon Johnson who became President of the United States went to a normal college in Texas and was a teacher. And a good one, by the way. There were thousands of school boards in those days. And the funding was inequitable. The foundation formula was just getting going. So, it was a time when you could teach with a year – some people were being trained for three or four months after grade 12 and then being put in classrooms in the fall. The demand was so great. But that changed. I remember it changing in the early '80s and then it became a requirement that anybody who did not have a bachelor's degree had to go back and get a bachelor's degree. And they were given assistance, but there was a time limit set, I think, of five years when everyone was expected to have a degree. So, it took a while for that to change.

But certainly, it was quite common to have, what they call, a license to teach or a teaching certificate with two years out of high school. That was common with the cohort that I was with.

## 2  Teaching up North in Yellowknife, NWT

After that first year, I decided for a number of reasons, not just the superintendent's message, but for a number of reasons I really wanted to have, I guess, an adventure and see different parts of the country. There were jobs all over Canada. I met my wife in January. We got married in July, and we both applied to go North and ended up in Yellowknife in September. She was an elementary specialist, and I was a secondary specialist. So, it was an opportunity to get back into the area that I was trained to teach. We were in the North which was quite different than any experience that I'd had. The Northwest Territories was one and three-quarter million square miles, the same size as India. And it had 30,000 people compared to almost a billion people in India… A huge area. I became president of the teachers' union and a member of the territorial executive responsible for professional development. I was responsible for bringing all teachers in the Northwest Territories into Yellowknife for a two-day conference every March which was a huge logistical undertaking. I was young and so it was a great experience to just organize the logistics and the planes and the billeting and so on that had to take place. And I got to know teachers from not only all over Canada but from all over the world when we had these conferences. We had leading-edge speakers. We had a territorial department of education who were young like we were.

We were really on the leading edge as far as curriculum and instruction were concerned. It's really where I first learned to differentiate instruction. We had a large significant number of Aboriginal people form whom English was not their first language. We had to have translators for parent-teacher interviews so that they could translate our English into Dogrib language so the parents could understand. We had a Dogrib village, that was across a portion of the lake from Yellowknife and the lake would freeze in the winter and the children would skate 15 miles to school over the ice. They were absent from school in the wintertime because they would be out on the land with their parents. That was expected. So that was all new to me. We decided to go with qualitative report cards which I know people are talking about now again with the competencies. So, I remember writing 12–14 pages for each of the 35 students in my class during report card time, without any marks. And there was a parent revolt when the report cards went out. So, there was a hasty retreat beaten on all sides and we were back with marks the following year… But with more of a qualitative type of description that stayed with respect to what students were doing.

We had great extracurricular activities. It was dark a good time of the year. So, you really had to make your own fun and we had again, a lot of first, second, third-year teachers. We played hockey and we put on a great musical, and we took it to Inuvik by plane and we toured the North with it. We would start playing baseball games at 10:00 at night and played all night... we would do things like that. So, it was a really great experience for a young teacher to have. Resources were not an issue, because the federal government was funding everything, so anything a teacher asked for they ended up getting. But another lesson I learned from that experience, although resources were no object, we were paid very well, and we were looked after very well. [Nevertheless], our results were very poor. So, I learned that it's never just a question of money; it's how the money is being spent... And especially if it's spent on improving instruction and working with teachers to improve instruction and improve teaching and learning. So, it was a lesson... I never saw those days again as far as unlimited money was concerned. But I certainly learned that there's never going to be enough money, but we have to be very strategic in the way we spend it.

Well, I learned that in the North we were removed from people below the 60th parallel. The only way you could get out of the North in the winter is you flew, and you had to fly in and there weren't any roads beyond Yellowknife. So, you could be fairly isolated. You had to be very creative in what you did. So, we had textbooks and money wasn't an object as far as textbooks were concerned. But it created another very significant issue for us, because many of the children we were teaching, did not see themselves reflected in the textbooks that we were using. They were Dogrib people. They were still living on the land. They still had their own language and culture. And it was very difficult for them to relate to Tom, Betty and Susan in middleclass America which were the textbooks we were using. So, the Department of Education in Yellowknife tried to get publishers to publish more textbooks that were more in line with what Canadians would see or Canadian children would see, but especially First Nations children would see. And they were not successful. So, they set up teams of teachers and we wrote readers and textbooks. And we had First Nations people do the illustrations. And those were the first readers that I saw and the first math books that I saw that were actually created within Canada. And they were created in the North and they were based on the various cultures in the North. So, we had all these funds to get what we wanted, but on the other hand, it wasn't really a way that a lot of the kids that we had could engage with the curriculum. I learned a lesson that you have to be resourceful, and you have to be creative. We had leadership that allowed us to be creative and innovative and allowed us to create materials that the children we had in our classrooms were going to relate to.

I think with the innovations we had in the North it was interesting that I think in the year I left, they terminated the people who were leading that initiative in the North. There certainly were Aboriginal people who spoke quite highly of these changes, but there was also a lot of resistance to it from other areas who thought we should have been using the regular textbook. So, you saw progress and then you saw areas where there were valleys and the progress stopped. And then, there was, I think, a period where there was status quo for a period, from my perspective. And then things really started to change, I think, rapidly after the Charter of Rights and Freedoms came and the constitution was patriated and people could, parents could, and various groups in society including teachers could, challenge the status quo. And then I think there was more rapid progress then in every area including special education and the rights of Indigenous people and a range of issues. Everything [has changed], from the way students dressed to corporal punishment and discipline and religious freedoms, freedom of expression, just a whole range of issues that have come before the court. So, I think progress was slow, up until that period of time. There was progress, but I think it really became more rapid after the repatriation of the Canadian Constitution.

## 3    Changes in Assessment Practices

When I graduated from high school in Nova Scotia, we wrote the provincial examination set by the Atlantic Provinces Examination Board. The exams were worth a hundred percent. Nothing you did, no assessments that were done on you between September and June counted. We got regular report cards at the end of each semester or at the end of each term. There were set pass and fail grades. But the provincial exam was worth a hundred percent in every subject. So, you were given a number. Teachers were not allowed to supervise the exams. They always hired people who were taking their BEds or people from the normal colleges would come in and supervise the exams. You were given a number. You were put in large classrooms with students from other high schools. So, they tried to make it as impersonal as they possibly could. And then if you had a bad day, you didn't get into university. You didn't get into post-secondary institutions. Everything was based on those exams. There wasn't a lot of choice. You took a standard curriculum – English, mathematics, history. You took one foreign language which could be French or Latin. You took chemistry and physics. All these subjects were mandatory and physical education was mandatory as well. And that's the provincial examinations. So that was the regime that I came through and it started to change when I started to teach.

Now we're at a point where we're eliminating, it looks like we're going to eliminate all provincial examinations [in BC]. Over the years we ended up with the examination being worth a portion of the mark, a large portion of the yearly mark, and then a much smaller portion until, in the last few years provincial examinations [in BC and elsewhere] are being eliminated altogether. Elementary schools, of course, had a similar type of regimen but it wasn't a provincial examination that was set. You had tests and you were kept back, and I remember students being kept back in the same grade for four years. I remember that vividly when I was a student. And those students would leave school, of course, by the time they ended up getting to grade 7. I remember in grade 8 we had 56 students. We had to write a city exam. We were in a very low socioeconomic area and I remember our teacher would bring us back, starting in January at night, two nights a week, and on Saturdays to teach us, to give us extra help and at the end of the year every one of those 56 students passed those city exams. And then as a result of that there was an investigation. They didn't believe that all 56 students from that school in Halifax could have passed the exam. There had to be some type of collusion or mistake. And I remember all of us being brought in and interviewed and I remember telling them that. They found it quite incredible that he would spend this time and bring us back at night and do all these things to make sure that we were going to pass these exams. So, it was quite a remarkable experience. But he was probably the best teacher I ever had, and he grouped students which nobody was doing in those days. We talk about changes in curriculum and so on. Grouping then became popular and we still do it to some extent, but we differentiate now on an individual basis. So, it was part of the progression. Assessment, exams, retention was predominant, and the more students were retained the more students dropped out. I think that was going on at the university, when I went on to university it was about 15%. Now, it's about 85 or 80%. So, we've come a long way and I think a lot of it is as a result of the person that knows best where students are is the classroom teacher. And so, we've changed from that impersonal type of system with the examination structure in some ways, all the way through the system, to a system now where really the teacher is the one that is mainly responsible for assessments. And it's differentiated and we have supports through special education and other supports for classroom teachers that will really help students regardless of where they are [in their learning] to reach their potential. So that's been a really remarkable change. And we're now, I think, though, on the precipice of what is probably one of the most exciting reforms that I've seen in my life, in my career in education. And that's the redesign of the curriculum, the advancement of technology, the integration of technology in classrooms and the redesign of the curriculum – The assessment based on competencies. I think it's just a wonderful reform and it's like a new revolution and I wish I was going to be around for another 20 years to be part of it. I think it's one of the most exciting things I've seen in my career.

CHAPTER 6

# Beverly: Rural Ontario to Europe (1972–2021)

Beverly grew up in Paris, a small town in rural southwestern Ontario. She lived on a five-acre hobby farm and attended a one room schoolhouse from grade 1 through 4. Beverly started her formal schooling in 1957. There was no kindergarten. Her first teacher was a seasoned veteran with more than 40 years of teaching experience. When she retired, her successor, a novice teacher, struggled but as Beverly put it, "we struggled together." From grade 5, Beverly was bused to a larger community school in Brantford. Then, she entered Brantford Collegiate High School in grade 9. Beverly had four siblings – two older brothers and two younger brothers. She was the only girl. It was the 1960s, and in those days, career choices for girls were rather limited. Generally, girls were not expected to attend school beyond grade 12. Her parents felt that "The boys had to be educated first." So, grade 13 and university were initially not in the cards. It seemed likely Beverly would become a nurse, which was a practical choice and did not require a university education at that time. One could enter a nursing college after grade 12 and "work" as part of their training. However, Beverly had teachers who thought otherwise and had other plans for her. One day, when Beverly returned home from school, she was surprised to see a couple of unfamiliar cars parked in the driveway. Two of her teachers and a school counselor had traveled a great distance to convince her parents to let Beverly continue with her schooling. One year later, they returned again to offer their financial support so that Beverly could go to university. With the support and encouragement from her teachers, Beverly was able to obtain university entrance scholarships. One teacher even took a computer science course with Beverly to encourage her to attend university. Beverly was the only girl in this class. Beverly learned Fortran and was offered a scholarship to Waterloo University to study computer science. But that was not her calling. Beverly loved English and math. She entered Trent University in Peterborough, majoring in English with a minor in math. But in her third year, she was not happy, as none of her classes piqued her interest. She wanted to do something else. After classes one day, she asked a friend with a car if he would drive her around town to explore her options. In Peterborough there were three post-secondary schools: a bible school, a nursing school, and a teachers' college. It was on that day that Beverly decided she wanted to be a teacher. Despite the fact classes had already started and she was a week late, Beverly was admitted into the teacher education program. She knew that day that this was her calling.

In teacher's college, one educational foundations course, Philosophy of Education, had a profound impact on Beverly's emerging teaching philosophy. It was 1972. Progressive education and new ways of thinking were permeating teacher education programs everywhere. Beverly's teaching philosophy was heavily influenced by the Hall-Dennis report, "Living and Learning" to go beyond the 3Rs to embrace the whole child. But she found there were big gaps between theory and practice. In her first year of teaching Beverly found that what she experienced in the classroom was quite different to what she had studied in teacher's college. Nevertheless, Beverly enjoyed her teaching. There was a strong sense of community. Her first job was teaching grade 7 in a community school. The parents were very supportive of teachers and the curriculum was clearly organized and prescribed. But there were no special education initiatives or education assistants, and lesson planning was challenging for a new teacher with little experience. In those days, children with mild learning disabilities or other challenges had little support, other than the classroom teacher. Moreover, there were 38 students in her class! Beverly spent many hours planning lessons in order to make them relevant, meaningful, and interesting, to help facilitate learning for her diverse group of students. Beverly taught grade 7 again in her second year of teaching. Beverly's second year went much better as she had a better understanding of the nature of her students and a strong foundation of curriculum, teaching and learning to build on.

## 1 Early Memories as a Novice Teacher

In Beverly's first year of teaching, a week before school started, the school principal asked Beverly if she would be able to "ring the bells" as she had a background in music, but she had no idea what he meant. Beverly imagined physically ringing a bell to signal the start of classes or perhaps playing a xylophone over the PA system. She was led to a room in a part of the school she had never seen before. Beverly was shown a coffin-like case that housed a set of handbells. These had been donated by the school benefactor's family 20 years earlier and had sat in this case unused for two decades. Apparently, the man for whom the school was named after was not only a well-known educator but was also quite the bell ringer in his day! And for the school's 20th anniversary celebration, the principal wanted the bells to ring, so Beverly was asked to lead this initiative. But she had no experience as a bell ringer and had to learn it from scratch. Beverly not only had to teach students how to ring the bells, but she had to teach herself! Moreover, she did not have an entire full scale of bells to work with, so Beverly had to transpose the music into keys that would work with only one flat or two sharps in a two-octave range of bells. This was the start of Beverly's work as a choir director and bell ringer – something she came to love dearly.

Another challenge from Beverly's first year of teaching involved something that stemmed from her car pooling to work with a male colleague who also taught grade 7, across the hall from Beverly. As this male teacher's car was in the shop for a week, he had asked Beverly to give him a lift as it was on her way to and from school. A nosey parent had witnessed Beverly picking up this fellow in front of his home in the early morning hours. Putting two and two together, this *good citizen* came to the conclusion there was something inappropriate going on and informed the school principal. About two weeks later, Beverly was summoned to the principal's office. In what was called "an unnatural relationship" the principal told Beverly if this alleged affair was indeed true, one of them would have to leave the school. This was reported to the superintendent and beyond. The parent had even phoned the school board office to voice her concerns. This story from Beverly's first year of teaching speaks to the moral and ethical norms of the early 1970s and how teachers were held to a higher standard. Rumours can spread very quickly and can have a devastating effect on a teacher's career. Fortunately, in this case, it was quickly dealt with and cleared up. But this troubling incident left its mark on Beverly as a young teacher. Beverly was disappointed that a parent would go to such lengths, to complain to the principal, and that she was made to defend herself. While this was quickly resolved, Beverly did not have the chance to resolve this with the parent who made the complaint. It remains unclear if the parent was ever told the truth about what happened. Also, this rumour spread throughout the school, the entire school district, and the wider community. Beverly's father who worked as a school custodian, even caught wind of this *shameful* incident. Needless to say, this was unfortunate. How would this be handled today?

On a happier note, in Beverly's third year of teaching, she was asked to teach math and language arts to a grade 8 class of 30 gifted children. It was 1976. These students were given IQ tests in grade 6 and offered this special learning opportunity. Only those students designated as "gifted" could participate in this special program. They were bused into Beverly's school from all over the district, so these students were not part of the school community when they entered her class. Beverly noted that these students did not know one another at all and were very competitive. There was an unhealthy learning environment at the start. Students were very jealous of each other. Everyone was comparing marks all the time. They would even try to sabotage each other's class work! Beverly was very concerned about these students. So, Beverly invested a great deal of time and energy at the start of the school year, to nurture a positive learning environment. The classroom culture changed dramatically as a result and they become a wonderful community of learners. The students learned to be supportive and acceptive of one another. In addition, during the year, in return, Beverly learned a lot about gifted students. These students were so bright, they pushed Beverly's learning curve… she was kept on her toes and was literally just a few steps ahead of them! It was a challenge to keep these gifted students actively engaged and challenged in their individual learning journeys.

## 2    Teaching Overseas (Germany, Belgium and the Gulf War)

In my fifth year of teaching, I applied to teach for the Department of Defence at one of their schools for military children overseas. To my delight I was chosen to go to Baden-Baden, Germany to teach in 1979–1981. It was quite the experience! Other than knowing that I had an uncle in the Canadian Army, I knew very little about the military culture. My grade 7 class had 32 students who had come from all over Canada. I quickly realized that different provinces and territories had different curriculums which meant that some topics/skills were not necessarily taught in the same year. I called these "black holes." Pre-testing was a valuable diagnostic tool for me to develop meaningful programs for each student. I also had students who had been failed one to three times! I was determined to remedy this. To keep curriculum standard the Ontario curriculum was adapted at the school which played well for me. Another surprise for me was early in the year when my students had chosen a partner to do a project. I told them they may have to get together outside of class time. One pair quickly came up to me to say they could not go into each other's apartment buildings (Private Military Quarters – PMQs) because their fathers were of different ranks. That was a shock! I realized that there was a "caste system." Different apartment buildings were designated for certain ranks. I quickly arranged time outside of classroom hours for students to work at the school.

The military definitely honoured education. Profits made from the grocery/household goods stores had a designated amount that went to support school programs. Because of that, I was able to take my students skiing for a week in Austria and to Paris for an educational exploration. It was amazing! During my time in Baden-Baden, I met my husband to be. He was a Major in the Canadian Air Force.

In 1989, my husband was posted to the Supreme Headquarters of the Allied Powers of Europe (SHAPE) in Belgium. We were returning to Europe, now with two sons ages 5 and 6. School at SHAPE was exciting. Over a two-block section of the base were numerous school buildings all for each country in the North

Atlantic Treaty Organization (NATO). There was no Canadian kindergarten, so one son went to the British School and the other attended grade 1 at the Canadian School. I was quickly picked up as a substitute teacher or visitor in many of the schools as they were excited to have a teacher teach their classes English. One of my favourite stories came from my son in the British school. He was asked to be a "Wiseman" in the nativity story. He came home very excited to tell me and when asked which one he was, he replied, "the one that brings francs and cents."

While in Belgium that year (1989), my husband went on a training course near the East Germany Border. While driving there, we heard on the radio that the Berlin Wall had come down. We saw many "East Germans" drive to the town we were in. We also took a small side trip to go into previous East Germany with our K-car. We emptied pubs and restaurants as people were so excited to see such a luxurious American car. This was the beginning of our "living history" moments. The following year we were posted to Baden-Baden, Germany. My husband was now a Commanding Officer and we lived on the Base. I was able to teach again and was pleasantly surprised to find that all the PMQs were now mixed ranks. Again, my classes went on amazing educational trips from skiing to staying at a Medieval Castle and Mill while studying Medieval Times. During our time there, our base had the first fighter, maintenance, and army groups in the first Gulf War conflict, and the first peacekeeping group into the former Yugoslavia. There are many stories to be told on how those events touched our students' and families' lives but that is for another time.

CHAPTER 7

# Bill: Secondary PE & Social Studies (1973–2015)

Bill was born in 1950, as the second son of eventually three sons of two very kind, considerate and fun-loving parents who had each grown up in the Marpole area of Vancouver and got married prior to his father going off to fight in World War Two. After the war, Bill's dad returned, and purchased a lot on 60th Avenue in Vancouver, only a few blocks from his parent's house. The home was unfinished when Bill's older brother was born in 1947, but the basement was livable. The large park at the end of the block had swings, teeter totters, monkey bars, a sand box, a concrete wading pool, an outdoor swimming pool with 3 metre and 1 metre diving boards, plus a community centre, as well as playing fields for soccer and baseball, and two tennis courts. It was the perfect spot to grow up for Bill or any other child who loved sports. The South Granville community was thriving and had many amenities. In addition to parks and recreation facilities, there was the library. The book mobile would park at 67th avenue and Oak Street each week and Bill's mom would walk the boys there to sign out books using their own library cards.

The elementary school was located a couple of blocks north of the family home and also had playing fields. There were lots of similar aged kids who often got together and organized competitions with whatever sports equipment people had. It was in these informal, unstructured games that reputations and personal identities were formed. In grade 3 (1959), Bill recalls that each student in the class were individually interviewed and tested using intelligence and aptitude measures by a couple of government officials. From that testing, some children were identified as having academic potential and that group would be kept together for three years with the same teacher who had a noteworthy education background, to accelerate the learning potential of the selected group. There is no doubt that the quality of instruction and high expectations provided a distinct advantage in preparing each of us for an academic future.

## 1 Physical Education as a Pathway to Teaching

Bill first had the notion of becoming a teacher, as a grade 9 student in 1964. They had counsellors come in as part of guidance which took time away from physical education (PE) activities, his favourite subject. Students were in a classroom with a guidance counsellor, and they were talking about the future and what kind of job you might want. Bill recalls, "that was probably the first time I had ever thought about that question." As a 13-year-old boy, he was stumped for an answer. Bill's dad was a carpenter, his grandfather and great grandfather had been carpenters, but his dad was adamant that none of his boys would be carpenters. Bill would attend university. Teacher seemed like a logical choice.

> And I thought at the time, PE teacher because how could that be bad? You're going to play your whole life; so, I'll be a PE teacher! And I decided at that point, that's the answer I gave him, and it was comforting that anytime anyone asked that tough question about what you're going to do, I had an answer. I was going to be a teacher. And luckily, teacher was a good answer because I enjoyed all 42 of those years teaching.

With a clear idea of what he wanted to do, Bill attended the University of British Columbia (UBC) completing a Bachelor of Education with teaching concentrations in PE and Geography. He was hired by the Kamloops School District 73 (SD73) in 1973 where he taught for the next 42 years. Bill spent most of his career teaching PE and Social Studies at the secondary level. When Bill and his wife started their family, he decided that it may be fun to spend all day with young kids, so he took advantage of an opportunity to transfer to an elementary school. Within a few weeks he recognized that secondary school was a much better fit for him. He managed to transfer back to a junior high school after that one year by working in a work study/ work experience program and a special education program for several years, even though he did not have any specific training in either of these specialty areas, before he managed to return to teaching PE and Social Studies. In the interest of maximizing job security in a time in which teacher layoffs were happening, Bill added Law 12, Geography 12 and Civic Studies 11 to his teaching assignments.

## 2      Changes in Curriculum, Teaching and Learning

In the 1970s, the curriculum guides were very general and that was touted as a strength. Bill remembers a professor at UBC, a social studies methods teacher, who explained to teacher candidates that a flexible and open curriculum allowed teachers latitude, to be creative within the subject area, and make things more interesting for students. Teachers were not to be tied to a textbook. So that was Bill's mindset as a beginning teacher. This flexible approach to curriculum, teaching and learning continued to frame Bill's teaching philosophy for years to come, but as time went on, the curriculum guides got more prescriptive and the prescribed learning outcomes, then, became tied to government exams. The necessity to ensure that your students were prepared for those exams took away some opportunities for creativity in developing an interest in the subject area for students. Accountability rather than learning became the focus of administration. In Bill's last ten years of teaching (2005–2015), he had to prepare his students for Social Studies 11, Civic Studies 11 and Geography 12 government exams. The government exams were driving the courses as teachers were pressured to cover all content that may be tested and have their students achieve results above a provincial average. There were few opportunities to veer from the mandated curriculum and the prescribed learning outcomes. These exams at grade 11 counted 20% of a student's final grade in a course and 40% for grade 12 courses, often representing the difference between gaining entrance into a university program. Bill was invited to participate as a member of a group of four teachers plus a mentor from the Ministry of Education tasked with creating the provincial exams for Civic Studies 11. The appointment involved writing, editing and reviewing three exams per year consisting of 55 multiple choice questions focused on knowledge and understanding based on the learning outcomes of the course plus two essay questions assessing higher level thinking skills. Bill continued on this team as an item writer, selecting exemplars to assist teachers in grading the essays and as a trial writer to assist with the final edits of the exams for several years. Bill is thankful the curriculum has changed.

With British Columbia's new curriculum (2021), gradually introduced in the mid-2010s, focused on core competencies rather than prescribed learning outcomes and assessments, the pendulum has swung decidedly back to a more holistic way of thinking. In Bill's words,

> I can see some similarity to the beginning [of my teaching]… It seems as if it's going to become more open to allow students input into the direction… just as it was in 1973 when [there was] flexibility for the teacher. [Back then], you knew what the curriculum was, the Ministry had assigned textbooks and you had latitude to move away from that textbook and use other materials. Although those other materials were difficult to acquire because there was no Internet and so you were depending on your own travel experiences or your own life experiences to try to see where that would help young students to understand certain concepts. And so, with the new curriculum it seems as if that opportunity will exist for teachers, but it'll also be extended to students who will be able to provide some direction as to what they're interested in learning. And I think together the teacher and the student will figure out how it's going to be something

that's important that's being studied… And not just something where a student is in their comfort zone and are not growing because they continue to just study, talk about and do the same project over and over. But [rather] that they genuinely have a thirst for knowledge and a powerful direction that they want to take their education.

## 3  Changes in Technology

Technology changed incredibly over the four decades of Bill's career. Chalkboards gave way to overhead projectors, whiteboards and then smart boards. Data projectors and digital media like YouTube replaced films, videos and DVDs. Teachers received little in-service training on how to use new technology in their classrooms. These were things Bill and others had to learn on the job.

> Well, in terms of technology I can remember before I graduated, taking a course in audiovisual components and learning how to thread a 16-millimetre projector… You then went on a practicum and felt pretty smart in front of a class that you could actually handle the threading of the film. But that only lasted a very short time and then film was not part of the curriculum and you were into other modalities. But I think the spirit master [notes], that was always something that you were preparing, and you were running those off for classes. To have a photocopying machine and the quality of those photocopies definitely improved connection for kids and made it easier. But then budgets started to change too. And you were told to not copy so many things and find another way. And the other way, then, wasn't yet to have students with their phones and using the phones, although in the last few years that I taught, then, that was more the structure in the classroom. You would maybe, in a law class, be talking about a particular case and, of course, you don't know every case. And students were able to find the case on the Internet and we could discuss something about the judgement and find out in real time, then, what our thoughts were about that judgement.

## 4  Changes in Assessment and Evaluation

Other significant changes that occurred over the four decades of Bill's career included assessment practices. This is a common theme mentioned by other teachers who started their careers in the 1970s. Bill noted that besides technology, one of the other major changes that he experienced had to do with grading, evaluation, and assessment of students.

> Around the issue of assessment... I know that changed quite a lot. In the beginning an assessment seemed to be fairly straightforward. I mean, people would talk about grading on a curve, and it wasn't something that was insisted upon in my experience. But it was something that seemed to kind of naturally happen, that you had a few students that would get an A. Another few students would get a B and you would have a large number of students that were in that C+, C, C– sort of category and then, again, fewer that would have a D and some that would have an E. And so that was the spectrum of the marking, and it did work out that way that it looked like a bell curve. And so maybe that was part of what we as students ourselves were used to and it just became part of what happened in the school setting, the high-school setting. And that changed. And sometimes I'm not convinced that it changed for the best. I think that while we moved into a recognition of formative and summative assessment and the benefits of offering students a chance to learn things before we were assessing them in a summative way, I think that got warped somewhat with this notion that failure is not an option. And that somehow someone not achieving an adequate standard was a terrible experience for them and something that we needed to avoid at all costs. When in fact, in my opinion, failure can be a good option. It teaches us something, right. It's not a dead-end. It's a chance to redo. It's a chance to do it better the next time. So, my concern is that I'm not sure how in the new curriculum assessment will be done without just sort of handing out marks and not really helping students understand that sometimes the questions that they ask themselves are questions they already know the answers to. Perhaps they are not taking risks. They are not growing, and therefore, they are not learning.

CHAPTER 8

# Anne: Music Teacher, Administrator & Professor (1984–)

Anne was born and raised in London, Ontario. She is the youngest of three girls but has one younger brother. Anne indicated that her family background had a great deal to do with why she chose to become a teacher. Anne's parents were both university-educated. Moreover, she has extended family members that rose to very high levels of education, including an uncle who worked at Los Alamos as a nuclear physicist and another family member who attained a doctorate and became a dean of education. When Anne was quite young, Anne's mother became a teacher to support the family. Anne loved music. Encouraged by her high school band teacher, she decided to study music at Queen's University. Then, she did a master's degree in music therapy. Anne's mother enrolled her in teacher education as she felt it was important to have a teaching certificate as a "way of earning a living." This was a pragmatic decision. Unfortunately, Anne's mother passed away far too young, and Anne was without both her parents in her mid-20s. While Anne might be considered middle class, the family had very difficult financial years due to her father's undiagnosed PTSD (WWII) during her formative years. Anne credits her band teacher with inspiring her. This teacher provided individualized 1:1 instruction, guidance and more. He was a great mentor.

## 1   Mentor: High School Band Teacher

Teachers often go into teaching as a result of a significant positive experience within their own formal schooling. Many teachers credit a specific teacher who inspired and motivated them to become a teacher. Anne's high school band teacher is a perfect example. He went above and beyond the call of duty, encouraging Anne to pursue music in post-secondary studies and more. Don Clarke was a Potsdam-trained musician of tremendous ability. He became a high school music teacher because it provided financial and other stability, not because he could not 'make it' as a gig musician or in an orchestra. Don's advice to Anne included "Do not go into performance in your music degree. It is unrealistic. You need to go to a university with a strong music education program, one that sees music education as its raison d'etre.

## 2  1980s Ontario Schooling: Religion/Class Considerations

Anne started teaching in 1984. There were very few opportunities for new teachers, and it normally took some time to find permanent work. She taught in a number of limited term contract positions, in urban and semi-urban settings of Waterloo, Ontario (pop. then was about 200,000 but now it is more than 700,000). Teaching provided a sense of independence and it was not far from home. The Kitchener-Waterloo area is rather unique. This region of South Western Ontario has some of the richest farmland in Canada. Interestingly, especially in this part of Ontario, there is a significant Mennonite population as well as a strong German ancestry. Mennonite elders held influence in educational decision-making. Horse and buggies are still in use by some people. Anne taught seven years in a variety of schools, before becoming an administrator. Then, Anne moved on to become an education officer in the Ontario Ministry of Education, and later, a program officer in the Ontario College of Teachers (OCT), and eventually a university professor in leadership. Anne had women mentors that supported her and encouraged her to go into leadership and administration.

## 3  Novice Teacher Stories of Experience

Like other new first year teachers at that time, Anne had a challenging potpourri of courses to prepare in her first teaching assignment. Furthermore, she taught at five different schools in her first four years of teaching. While vocal and instrumental music were always central, the rest of the teaching assignment consisted of a mix of classes in what is sometimes referred to as "a dog's breakfast." In her first year of teaching, Anne had six days of teaching with six different courses to teach, including grade 7/8 vocal and instrumental, grade 5/6 social studies, art, health, mathematics, and music. In addition, Anne was responsible for running the band program and choir. She also put on an impressive musical production of Annie. In the midst of her musical preparations, she broke her ankle, but she was only off work one day. While the principal thought the musical was a bust, Anne came to work, in a cast, propped her leg up on the piano stool and got to work! Anne knew that her first year of teaching was really important to landing a permanent position and to her career, so this was her chance to prove herself.

In Anne's first year, she had the opportunity to observe the vice-principal, a veteran teacher, teach the same group of students. During her prep period, she remained at her desk, while this other teacher taught guidance lessons to her grade 7 and 8 students. Anne watched this exemplary teacher effectively lead the class. It was an excellent learning opportunity and a noteworthy example of how teachers often learn a great deal serendipitously while on the job, through all sorts of means. This unique, unplanned situation offered Anne one of her most significant educational experiences, as a young, novice teacher. It helped to observe a strong teacher, and the subject matter invited deep understanding of adolescence. If this arrangement could be replicated somehow, it would be an outstanding way for all teachers to learn from their senior colleagues. Nevertheless, as Anne notes, the learning between junior and senior teachers is a reciprocal relationship, and often veterans learn a great deal from novices.

Anne's second limited term contract was teaching at a semi-rural school in Cambridge, Ontario. Anne staged another musical. She met a lifelong friend and mentor, Patti, the school principal. Patti later became the director of education. Anne credits Patti for nurturing her as a young teacher, and for early conversations about leadership. They became very close friends and have remained friends to this day. Anne even babysat for Patti while she travelled around the province as part of her work. Anne was like a surrogate mother or auntie to Patti's child. Watching this exceptional educator, with the depth of understanding of her personally, not only encouraged Anne in leadership undertakings over the years, but it also stabilized Anne as she experienced the death of her parents, marriage, and parenthood. On her teaching evaluation Patti recommended Anne should "Try to spend more time on your bulletin boards!" Principals often have to 'dig deep' to find improvement areas for exceptionally strong young teachers!

In her third year of teaching, Anne had to move again. She taught in two different schools. One was a typical suburban school while the other was in the core of the city. The contrasting realities of children was the learning. And it opened Anne's eyes to the gaps in language and the consequences of this for new immigrants to Canada, the learning effects that low socio-economic status may create, and how the focus of teachers sometimes shifts based on the learners in front of them.

Fortunately, in Anne's fourth year of teaching she was awarded a permanent teaching position. It was important that after several limited term contracts, she was finally secure in a full-time permanent teaching position. Anne learned a lot during these formative years of teaching.

> The constant movement of schools opened my eyes to a lot of things. It gave me an understanding of schools in an organizational sense. I saw a lot of principals. I saw a lot of staffs. I saw every grade and every subject.

Anne was able to continue her professional development by taking a number of courses in music education, special education, primary education and leadership. Also, another critically important development in Anne's experience as a novice teacher was that she was asked to join the bargaining team for the teacher's union. Anne was an active member of the Waterloo County Women Teachers' Association. Through that experience, Anne became chief negotiator for all the elementary teachers and administrators. Furthermore, she received provincial training in negotiations and conflict management. The opportunity to get out of the classroom, to observe a variety of educational settings, and to learn through these experiences is something that Anne credits for helping her to better understand the nature of teaching. Also, this was critically important in forming her emerging educational teaching and leadership philosophy.

One of the most rewarding aspects of her teaching job included the extra-curricular activities. She started a jazz choir made up of eight students in grades 7 and 8. There were four girls and four boys. The jazz choir focused on learning about four songs in four-part harmony. The boys, being at that awkward age of changing voice, had a very limited vocal range but the results were impressive, and this group quickly earned a reputation and following. There was another music teacher, Phil who was quite an accomplished pianist and he accompanied them on piano. In Anne's words,

> He could rock that piano… So, we got invited to go everywhere… The students were so proud of themselves. They actually became like heroes or minor celebrities in the school. We would perform in assemblies and we'd get invited to go places… It was fun and it was a great success.

## 4      Mentor: Veteran Teacher/Administrator/Principal/Friend

In Anne's fourth year of teaching, she finally got a full-time job at a new school, the same school as her most significant mentor and friend, Patti, who was now in her third principalship, and clearly had been earmarked for promotion in the future. Patti, eager to prove herself, created a timetable where Anne taught half the school's students at a time. Anne taught music to 200 children from grades 4–6 one day of the week for an hour on Wednesdays in the gym and then another 200 primary aged children the next day. This was not part of standard practice. It was highly unorthodox, but Anne did not know it at the time. It was only later that Anne came to realize that she was doing an incredible favour to the principal by taking on this challenge. The principal received accolades for group planning, but it was really Anne who was behind this success story. As Anne said,

I learned the hypnotic effect that music has on children... and that really good music teaching has a huge impact on children. I managed those music classes by myself, because I knew how to teach music... and they loved it... I remember teaching Dvořák's opening of the second movement of The New World Symphony, Me-So-So, Me-Re-Do... and you could have heard a pin drop... I changed lives in that class. Principals and coordinators from other districts were coming to my classes, something that had occurred in my first-year teaching because of my classroom management skills, but now they were coming from all over because of my music education skills. But nobody ever said, "Wow, Anne you're pretty good at this (other than her principal)." When I look back, if anybody had every told me I was that good, I would have been pleased..." It was an amazing experience for a young teacher, but as is often the case, there were few pats on the back. "A fine beginning..." was what one school leader said in his brief comments as part of my mandatory first year teaching evaluation. I was promoted to vice-principal. So, I was recognized eventually.

## 5    Words of Advice for New Teachers

While moving from school to school and having loads of different courses to teach as a novice teacher was very challenging, Anne noted that these were incredible learning opportunities. Changes and in particular changes that occur early in a teaching career are good things. So, doing supply teaching on limited term contracts is a strength rather than a weakness. Anne's advice for teacher candidates includes the following:

1. Never stop learning. Courses provide a means to have conversations with other teachers... This is quite different from PD days. Keep taking coursework.
2. If you can know your worth, that might be helpful.
3. Change is good. Although it was difficult changing schools, the learning was great!

CHAPTER 9

# Gloria: Rural Colombia to Urban Canada (1988–)

Gloria's remarkable story of experience takes us on a journey from rural Colombia to the United Kingdom, then to Toronto and finally to Thompson Rivers University, in Kamloops, British Columbia, where she lives and works now.

## 1   Colombia to the United Kingdom: Escuela Nueva and Early Teaching

Gloria was born to a large family of 14 children. They lived on a farm in the Andean region of Colombia. When Gloria was six years old, they moved to a town, where Gloria completed her elementary and secondary school education, which included teacher training. Back in the 1980s, in Colombia, it was competitive to become a teacher. Teachers were respected and highly regarded. Gloria was bright. She had the right personality traits to become a teacher. Gloria's family made the decision that she was to be a teacher. So, Gloria attended a typical *Escuela Normal public school* and started to prepare to be a teacher in grade 8. As a teenager, Gloria took courses like "Didactic Tools," "Philosophy of Education," "History of Education," "Curriculum," "Classroom Management," and "Ethics in Education." In addition, similar to our TRU teacher candidates, at age 14, she observed teachers in elementary schools and wrote reports. In grades 9 and 10, Gloria took more teaching courses such as "Child Development" and "Methods of Teaching" reading, writing, and the content areas. Also, she did micro-teaching and a long practicum, co-teaching as well as teaching independently. Gloria eventually taught one full afternoon every week. In grade 11, the final year of high school in Colombia, she participated in intensive practicum internships for two weeks at the beginning and end of the school year in the public schools in her town, and one full day per week during teaching units throughout the year. Gloria gained a great deal of teaching experience during these early days. Gloria graduated from high school with a primary school teaching certificate and degree at age 17.

She started her teaching career at the tender age of 17. Not everyone who entered school, was able to succeed. Gloria recalled another classmate, while very bright, she was too timid and according to the teacher educators, did not have the "right stuff" for becoming a teacher. Some students were encouraged to pursue other careers. Also, moral behaviour was watched carefully as this institution was run by nuns. Gloria was encouraged to pursue teaching. Her first job was as a primary school teacher for homeless children at a rural school, also run by nuns. Gloria recalled that she must have looked really young, in her first job as a teacher... "Is this a new student?" said the visiting psychologist. As a novice teacher, she motivated children who came from incredible poverty to persevere, to become literate and to better themselves. Students were brought to the institution by the police, when they found them ambling the streets, by social workers who worked in their communities, or by their parents, who somehow learned about the institution. Depending on the vulnerability (e.g., completely homeless) and moral or physical risk of the students (living in violent households or neighborhoods or at risk of being abused), the children lived at the institution or came daily and returned to their families at the end of the day. Some of them were orphans and were on lists for adoption; always a magic dream for them. Once students turned 18, they left the school. Some of them managed to become successful. Gloria remembers one of them; a child that first came to the institution with her mother when they were panhandling door to door. The nuns invited them in and persuaded her mother to sending her each day to the institution. The child was in a terrible state of malnutrition and was hospitalized a few weeks after her arrival. Gloria and the nuns feared and prayed for her life. She eventually recovered and remained at the institution until she graduated from high school. This little girl was keen to learn. Gloria recalled how while other students were enjoying playing in the pool, this student often chose to stay in and study. She completed two years of schooling in only one year and progressed quickly through her studies. Years later, when visiting her hometown, Gloria learned from a friend that this girl was an employee at her friend's firm. Gloria's protégé became an accountant! This story shows the power of education.

This little girl of about 8 or 9 came from a local shanty town and had been raised in appalling squalor. The home she lived in was nothing more than a shack made from scraps of metal and other materials at hand. While appearing weak, she had inner strength. The resilience of this child was amazing. Although they were uncertain of her age, because she did not have a birth certificate and they could not obtain reliable information from her mother due to her poor mental state, they suspected she was about 9 years old when she arrived. She had not attended school before, but she was an eager learner and quickly caught up. The flexible system of *Escuela Nueva* allowed her to progress from grade to grade at her own pace, which once she developed her foundational reading and writing skills, was fast. This was a story of success, but others were unable to overcome life's challenges. Some of them went back to the streets, became prostitutes or ending up dead. Gloria's story and the story of her students is one of hope and resilience.

While attending traditional schools in Colombia, Gloria was first introduced to *Escuela Nueva* on her extended teaching practicum in grade 11. It was 1988. Gloria observed small groups of students, working together in learning centres and teachers using innovative pedagogies at rural schools. These multigrade classrooms provided rich learning opportunities to a variety of children who received highly individualized instruction, as they were each at very different levels of language and literacy. This intrigued Gloria. It was very different to her own education thus far.

Students in *Escuela Nueva* move through learning centres at their own pace. These progressive new schools started in the mid-1970s and have spread from rural Colombia throughout Latin America and all over the world. There are more than 20,000 of these schools in Colombia now. A great deal of research has been done on the success of these institutions. They are in stark contrast to the crowded classrooms, rows of desks, didactic teaching and general organization of traditional schools in Colombia. There are still about 50–60 students in public school classes. Public schools are very different now and then compared with the *Escuela Nueva*. It is important to note however, that implementation of *Escuela Nueva* is not always successful due to poor infrastructure. Gloria travels to Colombia every year and spends time in rural schools through various research and educational consulting projects. She has been dismayed to see the conditions at some of these schools. Many of the buildings are dilapidated. Just one teacher, in most cases with very little training, runs the whole school and is responsible to teach from K-5. Moreover, the schools lack proper teaching equipment to create rich learning centres. As a result, the teachers rely solely on the teaching guides provided by *Escuela Nueva* and workbooks that the students use to work throughout the content areas. Gloria witnessed 3rd to 5th graders working independently throughout the whole day completing the activities in the workbook, while the teacher worked with the K-2 students, teaching foundational skills using traditional, teacher centred methods. This is quite a different picture from the envisioned *Escuela Nueva*, which in theory was practiced at these schools. When Gloria first visited three of the schools in rural areas of her town in 2012, there was not one single book apart from the *Escuela Nueva* booklets. They did not have a library or even a shelf with books that children could read to enrich their learning experience. She obtained funds from the Federation of Postsecondary Educators of BC through an international solidarity grant to purchase books for these schools and to implement a community and family literacy program. Gloria remains concerned about the poor application of *Escuela Nueva* teaching principles and philosophy in many rural schools across the country and the lack of infrastructure and support for the teachers. It seems that in many places, the model has been reduced to the use of the learning guides.

Gloria's teaching philosophy was heavily influenced by what she experienced as a novice teacher within *Escuela Nueva*. Smaller classrooms, with students learning at their own pace and individualized instruction characterize Gloria's early teaching experiences. It is safe to say that Gloria got to know her students very well during these seminal years of her teaching.

After teaching several years at the institution for homeless children, Gloria found a job at a private school with a more flexible teaching schedule that would allow her to pursue a Bachelor of Education degree in English and Spanish. This private high school was quite different compared to the school for homeless children she left behind. There were 20 students in a class (compared with more than double that in the regular public schools). The students were wealthy, and they were older. And yet, they had tremendous needs. This was a school that received children expelled from other private schools because of their poor academic performance or behavioural challenges. The behavioural challenges were unbelievable. Some were using drugs, and part of her teaching duties were to supervise them during recess time to prevent them from using drugs at school. They constantly challenged her and called her the Drug Enforcement Administration (DEA) agent. "Oh, here comes the DEA!", they would shout. These were difficult students! She even received death threats once for not willing to change the final grade for a student, a very wealthy and troubling boy who at 16 was driving expensive cars and came to school with a bodyguard.

Working full time as a teacher while completing her Bachelor or Education (BEd) degree meant long days. She studied before and after school. Gloria would awake before 6 am, to study and then taught from 8:00 am until 5:00 pm. Then, Gloria would, take night classes from 6:00 to 8:00 am. She was so tired that on one occasion she fell asleep while teaching! But with early morning studies, energetic students, and evening classes, perhaps that is not surprising.

In 1996, she was hired, along with a team of British and Colombian educators to start a new private school. This was a bilingual school created with ambitious innovative goals. Gloria worked for several years at this elite private bi lingual school. It was in great contrast to her first teaching experience in a rural school but these early experiences as a novice teacher are just as significant to her teacher acculturation.

## 2    The United Kingdom to Canada: Opening Doors through Graduate Studies

With her Bachelor of Education degree in hand, with a focus on language and literacy, and strong desire to improve her English skills, in 1998, Gloria decided to study abroad. The United Kingdom (UK) was a natural choice. "I was not proud of my English." "I admired British culture, so I went to England." While taking advanced English as a Second Language (ESL) classes in London, she was able to get a job teaching at a daycare and was soon promoted to teaching kindergarten and then to becoming the coordinator. Gloria taught at this institution for two years. It was a good fit for her background in language and literacy. She remembers fondly the time spent with many children she taught at this formative age. Also, Gloria obtained a certificate from the Montessori Institute in London on teaching English as a second language to children.

It was during her time in the UK that Gloria started to dream about doing graduate studies. Gloria considered graduate programs in language and literacy offered in Australia, Canada, England, and New Zealand. England was deemed too expensive. The United States of America (USA) might seem an obvious choice to some, but Gloria was dead set against attending any universities in the USA, widely known as a hegemonic colonial nation and often not the best choice for international students. Gloria chose Canada, which seemed like a safe choice.

In August 2000 Gloria entered the Ontario Institute for Studies in Education at the University of Toronto (OISE/UT). Gloria's initial plan was to get master's degree and return to Colombia. She did not want to do a doctorate as an international student, as that would have been too expensive. One reason Gloria later decided to pursue a doctorate was that she realized she was not going to be able to be a public-school teacher in Canada without having to enter a Bachelor of Education program. The Ontario College of Teachers would not recognize her credentials. She would have to start over! Issues in degree transfers included all sorts of bureaucratic hurdles. For example, the universities in those days in Colombia, did not have detailed course outlines stored electronically. But as Ted noted in his *teacher-to-teacher conversation* with Gloria, "teaching is teaching!" Gloria insists she "developed way more skills" in her years of experience than Canadian students in an extended practicum.

During Gloria's graduate studies at OISE/UT, she realized that she was not going back to Colombia. She said that she became fully "acculturated" or "assimilated" into Canadian life in those years. Gloria lived in Toronto for nine years while completing her Master of Education (MEd) and Doctorate (PhD). During this time, Gloria taught Spanish classes at UT and worked as a research assistant under the supervision of a renowned scholar in language and literacy at OISE/UT. Soon after starting her graduate studies, she applied for residency and decided to stay in Canada. Residency status opened another door for her. Gloria has lived in Canada for more than two decades now, but she has great empathy for international students, having experienced it first-hand.

CHAPTER 10

# Ted: Transcultural Teacher from Canada to Japan (1989–)

Ted (the author of this book) was born and raised in Victoria, British Columbia, Canada. Throughout his many years in Canada and more than a decade in Japan, he learned a great deal through formal, informal, and non-formal education experiences. These transcultural experiences shaped his comparative education research, teaching philosophy and pedagogy in profound ways. Ted's story is focused on his early years as a novice teacher and his academic journey from secondary science teacher in the 1990s, to teacher educator two decades later.

## 1        Formal Education: The Road to Teaching and Academia

As both my parents went to The University of British Columbia (UBC), I naturally aspired to do the same. I obtained a BSc (Physics) degree in 1988 and subsequently enrolled in the Secondary Teacher Education Program at UBC. You could say I *fell into* teaching after several years of experience tutoring science and teaching clarinet privately. As I progressed through my physics major, I chose to take a number of elective courses outside the department. These included music composition, music history and creative writing. While others took these courses as required by their respective departments, I took them primarily out of interest. I preferred a broad, liberal education to a narrow, specialist course of study. However, in fourth year I began to wonder just what I would do upon graduation. It became obvious to me that an undergraduate degree in physics would not lead directly to any jobs in the field. I was told that I would have to get further training. So, I weighed my options carefully. I could continue to study physics and pursue a Master of Science degree, but I recoiled from the thought of spending all my days in a lab with little human contact. I envisioned myself becoming a reclusive, introverted and socially deprived single man growing old alone. After a summer of underemployment working in construction side-by-side with high school students, I was ready for a career move. All it took was a phone call from my physics lab partner asking if I had given any further thought to becoming a high school physics teacher. Almost on a whim, we had both applied to this program as a backup in case the job interviews and graduate school applications didn't pan out. As there was a shortage of physics teachers, I figured this would be a quick route to a well-paying job with lots of vacation time for other pursuits. I looked at teaching as a means to an end. Perhaps I could build on my teaching experience to become a lawyer or businessman. At the very least I would travel abroad to teach English while I sorted out my life.

While my lab partner and I both entered teacher education, he didn't survive the practicum and decided teaching wasn't his calling. I stayed on but had doubts about teaching as a lifelong career. My practicum progressed rather well, or so I thought, as I taught in basically the same manner of my high school science teachers, while trying to incorporate what I had learned in teacher training. However, I was given very little guidance from my sponsor teacher and I rarely saw my faculty advisor. Somehow, I was expected to know how to plan and implement original lessons, to effectively manage classes and to carry out the daily routines of teaching. Moreover, I was not given any feedback until the very end of the practicum, when I was told what I had been doing *wrong* and which areas needed to be further improved as I began my teaching career. This practicum experience gave a whole new meaning to the well-known *sink or swim* cliché of teacher induction. Essentially, my pre-service teacher education and extended practicum, while progressive and informative did not adequately prepare me for the challenges of teaching high school students.

I passed the practicum and upon graduation was immediately hired as a teacher on call (TOC) in Surrey, the same school district I did my practicum in. This is the usual way for beginning teachers to *get their foot in the door* as many school districts only hire directly from their TOC lists. I received a phone call on the first day of school to teach senior physics and biology as a teacher had taken a sudden leave of absence with no indication as to when he would return. I taught the classes as if I would have them the entire year, but I fully expected the return of the other teacher at any time. As days turned into months, it became clear that he was not returning. My temporary position eventually became a continuing permanent contract at 70% full time equivalency. I had three blocks of Physics 11 and two blocks of Biology 11. While I was well prepared to teach the physics curriculum, I had no training whatsoever in biology! In fact, I had never taken a biology course above Science 10. Consequently, I began to rely on the help of seasoned veteran biology teachers to show me everything from how to dissect a crayfish to how to operate a film projector. The mentorship of these teachers was essential to my survival that first year. As a part-time teacher, I had no homeroom, only two classes to prepare for, and three spare blocks instead of the usual one block and still, I was swamped with work! Most first-year teachers have to teach seven out of eight blocks with up to seven different classes to prepare for in addition to taking on a homeroom, coaching and other expected duties. I consider myself fortunate as a first-year teacher to have had sufficient time to plan as well as the expert guidance of experienced teachers, however it took me a number of years before I really became an effective teacher.

## 2 Teaching Abroad for Personal and Professional Growth

Having heard about teaching opportunities in Japan, I was enthusiastic about leaving my high school teaching position for new challenges abroad. In September 1990, I took a leave of absence and left Vancouver to venture across the Pacific to Tokyo, in an endeavor to achieve professional development and personal growth. I managed to get a job teaching English for the Shinjuku and Toshima School Districts. I stayed in Japan for two years. Moving back to Canada in 1992, I returned to teaching science in Surrey School District until June 2001. During this time, I took advantage of many professional development opportunities in an effort to improve my teaching. These included workshops on curriculum, classroom management, assessment strategies and other in-service programs. For three years as science department head, I had the chance to interact with teachers and administrators from all over the district. I had several student teachers and in my final year I volunteered as a mentor teacher for a new mentoring program for beginning teachers. I was happy to be able to give something back to the profession and to collaborate with new colleagues. However, I was disappointed at the low turnout from potential mentors and mentees alike. In the largest school district in British Columbia, with several thousand classroom teachers, I was paired up with the only other science teacher that chose to sign up for the program. I suspect the reason for this poor participation is that teachers do not have the time to attend these after school in-service sessions and they do not see the value in these initiatives. These experiences have given me great empathy and interest in teacher induction as this is an area, I think drastic improvements are necessary in the Canadian context. There is much to be learned from Japan's teacher acculturation. This became the focus of my doctoral research.

In 1995, while taking courses in language education at UBC, I became more and more intrigued with academic research relating to the sociological implications of education. While conducting research comparing Japan and Canada's junior high schools, I realized the significance of my unique experience and decided to pursue a Master of Arts (MA) degree in Educational Studies focusing on Canada and Japan's educational systems. Through attending comparative education conferences, presenting papers and writing my master's thesis, I decided to pursue a doctorate. My dissertation built on my experience, the comparative study in my MA thesis and the academic coursework of my program of study at the University of Toronto. Perhaps the most significant event in my first year of the program was the collaborative effort summarized in the following section.

## 3   Lessons in Collaboration – Teacher-to-Teacher Conversations

A serendipitous gathering of five unique graduate students on the first day of classes led to the formation of a curriculum, teaching and learning team. DO-AS-a-Team – Dianne, Odilia, Alison, Shijing, and Ted joined together to investigate notions of teaching within the contexts of their personal practical knowledge and the great educational philosopher, John Dewey. This journey of self and group-discovery was facilitated through a process of weekly meetings, extensive email discussions and a lengthy transcribed interview among the five members. Perhaps the word "interview" should be replaced with a more appropriate term such as conversation or dialogue.

The feminist interview methodology chosen enabled each participant the opportunity to contribute to the dialogue as well as the subsequent reporting of the findings. A transcription of the taped interview, complete with dialogue, field notes and reflections were supplied to everyone for verification. This proved to be a significant reliability check as several errors were uncovered. The taping combined with field notes and the ongoing email and face-to-face discussions provided a rich soil for cultivation of ideas. Each team member took on the task of writing different sections of a paper presented at a conference. These sections were then emailed to others for suggestions and comments. Next, the sections were pieced together, a summary was composed, and the entire document was further edited as a whole. Finally, a draft was emailed to all members and returned for final revisions. While this proved to be an arduous and time-consuming process, it was highly successful in integrating the diverse reflections of the five members into a single, coherent and meaningful paper.

Through our *teacher-to-teacher conversations*, we learned how essential it is to develop a rapport with the participants and to choose an appropriate environment for capturing their narratives. Researchers must take care to be culturally empathetic and to be aware that various cultures use communication differently. The use of native language, the choice of a non-threatening and comfortable setting, and the use of different registers can influence the outcome of an interview. Taping, in concert with field notes followed by extensive discussion for clarification, proved invaluable for recovery and reconstruction of meaning.

Dewey's (1938) notion of education and experience are timeless and cross-cultural in nature. His theories of learning have had a significant impact on each of us within our own conceptual framework and cultural context. Moreover, through the process of narrative inquiry and reflecting on Dewey situated within our own conceptions of teaching, we influenced each other to a certain extent. In addition, we came to terms with our own theories of teaching. We brought to the surface our deeply held beliefs and our tacit personal knowledge of curriculum, teaching and learning.

The richness of our collective thoughts illustrates the power of collaboration. It is somewhat ironic that many Canadian teachers often incorporate cooperative learning in their classrooms but seldom collaborate with colleagues. In their substantial daily routines and hectic schedules, teachers rarely have the opportunity to carry on a dialogue such as the one that transpired in our *teacher-to-teacher conversation*. It's a shame that our education system in Canada does not offer a means for collaboration and communication among teacher colleagues. Teachers must be given opportunities to learn from one another and to benefit from the accumulated wisdom of generations of skilled practitioners. Moreover, teachers must be given adequate time for collaboration, planning and reflection in order to grow as professionals. Experience is education. Teachers are first and foremost learners. Researchers, policy makers and practitioners must recognize that any effort to reform the structure or organization of schooling must foster teachers' personal practical knowledge, since education ultimately depends on the effectiveness of the teacher.

## 4 Educational Philosophy for Integrated Learning

I have always had a strong desire to learn, and I feel passionately about curriculum, teaching and learning. As a student, parent and teacher various educational experiences have shaped my constructivist teaching pedagogies and interdisciplinary educational philosophy. Subjects shouldn't be learned in isolation. Listening, speaking, reading, writing activities should be integrated and connected to students' prior knowledge and experiences. It is important to recognize that learning is based on lived experiences within both formal and informal educational settings.

In addition to the aforementioned, there were a number of other events that formed my approach to teaching. Firstly, in elementary school, I participated in a convergent/divergent thinking program and I conducted an original experiment that failed to prove my hypothesis but nevertheless won second place in the science fair. These opportunities for experimenting and exploring science in-depth, led me to major in physics and later to become a science teacher. One of the classes I enjoyed teaching the most was integrated Math/Science 8. I got a great deal of satisfaction making relevant connections to students' lives and showing the interconnections of subjects to their worlds. For example, when I asked students "What is $\pi$?" many responded, "3.14." But if probed further, to explain the meaning of $\pi$ most merely stated an equation like $A = \pi r^2$ or $C = 2\pi r$. I encouraged students to think critically by questioning, how to verify these equations and prove that $\pi = 22/7$ (approximately 3.14). Of course, if students are encouraged to construct their own circles and to measure the ratio of circumference to diameter, rather than simply memorizing equations and plugging in numbers, without thinking about the meaning, they can discover that the ratio is exactly 22/7. This fact can be extrapolated to explain how the Egyptians used trundle wheels to build their pyramids with astounding accuracy. In this way, math, science, history and other subjects can be successfully integrated into educational foundations classes. Thus, in my teaching, I try to make connections between various subjects, including math, music, social studies, and science, while introducing teacher candidates to critical thinking, global citizenship and social justice issues (see Howe, 2018a, 2018b).

Lifelong learning is an integral part of my educational philosophy. During the early years of my teaching career, I became increasingly interested in making contributions beyond the classroom. I sought out leadership and mentorship opportunities. Professional development became one of my most important activities. While teaching high school I enrolled in Teaching English as an Other Language (TESOL) courses, which became a catalyst for graduate studies. I began to attend international conferences and became further motivated to contribute to society through original research. In particular, my experiences within Canadian and Japanese classrooms led to my research interests in teacher education and comparative and international education. Thus, my MA thesis was a comparative study of Canadian and Japanese teachers' conceptions of critical thinking and my doctoral research was a reflexive ethnography of Japan's teacher induction. As a student at the Ontario Institute for Studies in Education at the University of Toronto (OISE/UT), my professional development was further enhanced. I thrived being in an environment surrounded with other enthusiastic educators. We learned together through our shared experience. Moreover, I learned a great deal about curriculum, teaching and learning from Michael Connelly, a renowned scholar in narrative inquiry. This solidified my progressive educational philosophy to incorporate teachers' personal practical knowledge and current notions of educational psychology like Gardner's multiple intelligences and Cole's socio-cultural theory. My philosophy also exemplifies Dewey's notion of experience and education summarized in the Confucian proverb, "I hear – I forget, I see – I remember, I do – I understand." Furthermore, cross-cultural learning experiences have enriched my classroom teaching while fostering empathy for multicultural learners. Leading by example, I strive to develop learner-centred lessons incorporating a variety of instructional strategies to actively engage and challenge students to think and express themselves.

CHAPTER 11

# Vessy: SOGI (Sexual Orientation & Gender Identity) Leader (1996–)

Vessy was born in 1970 to parents who immigrated from small remote villages in Northern Greece. She grew up in Oshawa, Ontario, about 60 km east of Toronto. Vessy has three brothers who were not well served by their schooling. Greek was spoken at home. So, Vessy and her brothers were all English Language Learners (ELL) and received very little English outside school. Vessy comes from a low-socioeconomic status and highly disadvantaged family. Her parents did the best they could, given the difficult circumstances but it was not the most ideal household to be raised in. Thankfully, school was a safe haven from her poor home life. "School was my safe space… I looked up to teachers as my role models." Vessy's story is one of strength and resilience. She overcame incredible odds to become a nationally ranked athlete, a successful teacher, and a highly respected school administrator. There are no other university educated siblings nor are there any teachers in her immediate family. However, Vessy indicated that she always wanted to be a teacher or a police officer. Vessy credits her teachers for inspiring her to further her education and to become a teacher. Teachers provided good role models. In fact, Vessy had some incredible teachers and mentors who went well above the call of duty. Extra-curricular connections like sports were very important to Vessy as a teenager. In particular, Vessy mentioned two teachers: D, who sponsored the photography club and was Vessy's teacher in grade 7 and 8; and L, who was a coach and physical education teacher. D spent a lot of time after school, helping Vessy and other students. In addition, L helped Vessy in so many ways. For example, L provided life lessons, connecting Vessy to others in the community and helped to find work for Vessy. Vessy babysat for L. She also cut the grass and did odd jobs for L and other friends of L. Vessy credits L for inspiring her to pursue teaching physical education and to play field lacrosse competitively.

## 1   Coaching and Competitive Sports: A Pathway to Teaching

"Most of my student loan went to my pursuit of the national field lacrosse team." Vessy made the national team but she also made her education a top priority. Vessy studied physical education and psychology at York University in the concurrent education program, obtaining her Bachelor of Education (BEd) degree in 1995. While Vessy was aiming for secondary teaching, every Thursday she went to an elementary inner-city school on a practicum. Vessy found it very challenging managing her grade two class, but it was a great learning experience. Vessy indicated that arts and crafts, reading, and other primary lessons were definitely outside her "wheelhouse"! Vessy lived in residence, so she was able to connect with other teacher candidates to share teaching ideas. Vessy was really challenged to find creative lessons to engage her young students. Vessy did not get much help from her faculty advisor or teachers. Fortunately, other teacher candidates in residence helped her to come up with lessons. Soon thereafter, Vessy and a close friend bicycled across the country through the United States to Vancouver, British Columbia (BC). It was an incredible journey. Along the way, Vessy and her friend met many generous people who restored her faith in humanity. Also, this experience gave her a lot of time to think and to reflect. Also, she has a "whole new appreciation for inclines" now! Arriving in Vancouver, six weeks later, Vessy found some work. Vessy has stayed in BC, ever since. Vessy missed the four seasons and Vancouver life did not agree with her, so Vessy hoped on a Greyhound bus and headed to Kamloops. She has called Kamloops home ever since. She began her teaching career as a Teacher Teaching on Call (TTOC) in the fall of 1996. Vessy's first teaching assignment was teaching part-time. While she was comfortable teaching physical education, she had one block of Science 9 and that was a challenge! Vessy was too shy to ask for help from her science colleagues. Then, in 1999, Vessy got her first permanent teaching position and moved to Barrier where she taught social studies there for six years. At this time, permanent teaching jobs were not easy to get. So, novice teachers had to accept positions in rural schools to get started. So, a number of new teachers car-pooled together from Kamloops to Barrier. These teachers formed a core group of individuals who chose to stay for more than the typical several years. Rather than the usual constant attrition of teachers in this rural school, during this period, there was some stability. Vessy became a coach and athletic director. Vessy was drawn to leadership. At this time, Vessy was an informal leader of the school. She had an excellent relationship with the vice-principal and the principal. Also, Vessy was a member of the Canadian Women's National Field Hockey team and then a few years later, as a coach she had the chance to work with other national level field hockey coaches, where she learned a great deal of leadership skills. Vessy loves working as a team. Coaching, teaching and leadership seem to go hand in hand. So, it seemed a natural career progression, when Vessy became a vice-principal in 2005–2006. While many young teachers only stay a short time in rural schools and tend to move on after only a few years, Vessy spent six years in Barrier before moving to Kamloops, where she became a principal and eventually a district administrator.

## 2 Mentoring of Teachers

Mentoring is an important element of teaching that Vessy feels should be implemented more explicitly. While Vessy did not have a significant mentor as a novice teacher, as an administrator, she always made this a priority for her new teachers. When Vessy started teaching, there was nothing in place for new teachers. Now, novice teachers get some help but there is still room for improvement. Vessy wishes there was a formal mentoring program to assist new teachers. It is something she hopes to change. Ironically, when Vessy started teaching, if there were issues, a meeting was called. Teachers would address it directly. Now, it is harder to do that. There is more bureaucracy. While Professional Learning Communities (PLCs) exist, it can be more challenging to tackle issues head on. Moreover, new teachers have been told to "take care of yourself" so, they are less likely to take on additional responsibilities. The focus is more on teaching. Students are less likely to have a teacher who goes beyond the classroom to inspire in the way Vessy's teachers did. For example, when the veterans retire, new teachers don't step up to do the coaching, sponsoring clubs. These roles are now often community members rather than teachers. But Vessy feels it is important to get to know students outside the classroom. So, this is something she would like to change.

## 3 SOGI (Sexual Orientation and Gender Identity) Leadership

Another priority for Vessy is SOGI (Sexual Orientation and Gender Identity). Vessy is the SOGI leader in the Kamloops School District. There have been many improvements in anti-racist, anti-bullying, and inclusive education. Over the past three decades, Vessy has seen lots of changes since she started teaching. In particular, over the past few years, much progress has been made. For example, the first Gender, Sexuality Alliance in the district was formed in 2006–2007 when she was a vice-principal at the time. Only since 2016, did gender identity get added to human rights and then the Ministry of Education included it in their mandate. Vessy has been a strong advocate for SOGI and is a district leader in inclusive education. While Vessy married and had a child, she came out as a gay woman while she was working as a vice-principal. Vessy was concerned about how this might impact her bid for a promotion to principal. Back in 2007–2008, it was still an impediment to advancement. This was especially true of smaller blue-collar towns like Barrier and Logan Lake and to a certain extent is still true today. Vessy has worked at larger urban schools like South Kamloops High School and Brock Middle School but she has spent a significant amount of her time at smaller rural schools such as Barrier and Logan Lake. These are very different contexts with different communities. Parents react differently to SOGI initiatives. Vessy recalled that when meeting parents, some of them questioned the need for SOGI orientations and one parent said, "Are we doing that SOGI stuff again this year?" So, many parents are not comfortable with SOGI in the curriculum at all. One parent said to Vessy, "You gays are a lot of fun… and you should be allowed to marry… and be as miserable as the rest of us!"

Vessy has been with her wife for 13 years but she only got married in 2017. "As a teacher in the 1990s, I would not have had the guts to come out." But I would hope now, things are different. Vessy came out years later when she finally was honest with herself about her sexual orientation. At first, she shared with close friends only. Vessy was worried that an openly gay person might not be accepted as a principal. Moreover, Vessy did not feel the school board trustees would approve as they were not supportive of the SOGI Social Justice 12 curriculum. "You need to come out several times." In a small town like Logan Lake "I want that community to get to know me based on the job I do, not my sexual orientation…" So, as principal of Logan Lake, she hid her identity at first. "People ask what you did on the weekend?" Vessy would carefully craft her responses to these questions with "We went to…" But eventually Vessy would say "My partner and I… *She*…" Vessy notes that in retrospect, for the most part, people did not care.

Nevertheless, there is still a double standard in our school systems, when it comes to sexual orientation. Vessy divorced her husband and then got remarried to her female partner in 2017. She recalls that at the time, a senior administrator took her aside and said that he would not be formally mentioning this at the next district meeting as he respected her privacy and didn't want to embarrass her. Interestingly, the following year when another male (heterosexual) colleague got married, it was announced and celebrated. Vessy feels this still reflects some people's awkwardness and difficulty accepting LGBTQ members of society. But recently, there have been welcome signs some positive changes. School board trustees are now participating in gay PRIDE parades and there is a great deal more support from the public. One of the things Vessy is most proud of is the great visible support from leaders within the Kamloops School District. Whether you are gay or straight, it is a great time to come out and support others in the LGBTQ community.

CHAPTER 12

# Alicia: Inclusive Special Education Entrepreneur

Alicia grew up in Victoria, BC. At the age of ten, in grade 5 she was stricken with a serious illness and was hospitalized. Her teacher at the time, Mrs. H. was compassionate, caring and went above and beyond the call of duty to provide Alicia with extra attention. Alicia credits Mrs. H. for opening her eyes to the difference a teacher can make in the lives of children. Alicia and Mrs. H. share a love for helping disadvantaged kids. They also both share a passion for art. There are many teachers in Alicia's extended family. So, perhaps it is not surprising that she chose this profession. However, it was not her plan to become a teacher when she entered university. Initially, Alicia was enrolled in the Faculty of Science at the University of British Columbia (UBC) as she loved biology and nature studies. But she soon discovered that science was not for her, so Alicia switched over to arts. Alicia majored in art history and graduated from UBC with her Bachelor of Arts degree in 1992. Upon graduation, she was still unsure about what she wanted to do as a career. Her first job was working in a framing shop. She knew that was not her calling but it paid the bills and at least she was connected with the art world.

Alicia has always enjoyed arts and crafts. As a child, she was always making things. In her twenties, she became a proficient potter and painter. Her artwork often had themes that embraced childhood whimsy. As art was something that brought solace and satisfaction to Alicia, she considered art therapy as a career, but her mother convinced her to get a Bachelor of Education degree instead. Teaching seemed like a more practical choice. Alicia also noted that most of her work and volunteer experiences involved some form of teaching. From private tutoring to providing nature tours, Alicia reasoned teaching was her niche. Also, teaching was a career that combined Alicia's talents in art with her desire to help disadvantaged children. Alicia's own struggles with social anxiety and the help she received from Mrs. H. strongly shaped Alicia's views and her educational philosophy. Moreover, given the fact that there are many teachers in Alicia's extended family, it seemed natural for her to also become a teacher.

Alicia entered the UBC Elementary Teacher Education Program in 1998 with the goal of making a difference in the lives of disadvantaged children. Alicia was keen to teach children with special needs. However, what transpired in her long practicum nearly derailed her plans to become a teacher. Fortunately, Alicia prevailed and graduated with her BEd (Elementary) in 2000.

## 1     Practicum Experience: Sink or Swim?

Alicia's long practicum was a traumatic experience. It was very stressful, especially towards the end. What happened? She still does not understand. One thing is for sure – Alicia did not receive adequate support or guidance from her faculty advisor or sponsor teacher. For the most part, she was left to her own devices. It was the classic training of "sink or swim" where Alicia was just thrown into the water without a life preserver or any tips on how to keep afloat. Part of the problem stems from the fact there are hundreds of students in the teacher education programs at UBC. Each faculty advisor is responsible for many students. This leaves little time for 1:1 guidance. So, a great deal of responsibility is placed on the classroom sponsor teacher. Without adequate support, student teachers are bound to fail. As was the practice in those days, Alicia was placed in small cohort. The two advisors (one man and one woman) divided up the cohort so that each of them had the responsibilities for about 10–12 student teachers. Things might have turned out differently for Alicia if she had been placed with the other faculty advisor but unfortunately, that was not in the cards. Problems with the male faculty advisor became evident in the midst of the practicum. He was curt, rude, nasty and had a difficult personality. Some students felt targeted and picked on. Alicia and others filed a complaint to the UBC Ombudsman, but it did nothing to help them through this difficult time.

    To make matters worse, Alicia had a very challenging classroom to manage. And it was an inner-city school. Student teachers were matched with sponsor teachers, based on grade level and other considerations. Alicia was matched with an older veteran teacher who taught grade 1. It was a challenging class with about half the students English as their second language (ELL) and a number of behavioural issues. Her sponsor teacher's ineffective method was to simply have Alicia observe and to use trial and error in her lessons with little advice. There was little dialogue or discussion. There should have been a great deal more reflection and *teacher-to-teacher conversations*. In the middle of the day, close to the end of the practicum, the faculty advisor took Alicia aside and said "you are in danger of failing…" It came as a complete shock to Alicia. The faculty advisor did not provide advice or constructive criticism – Nor did the sponsor teacher. Alicia described this situation as intensely traumatic. Clearly, it was a toxic environment at the school and a very poor way to start a teaching career. What Alicia saw behind the scenes during her practicum was not uplifting and it made Alicia re-think teaching in public schools. While all the teacher candidates in her cohort "passed," some, including Alicia, did not receive glowing letters of recommendation. So, it was nearly impossible for these teachers to get placed on teacher on call (TOC) lists (Note: while TOC is sometimes used and TTOC for "Teacher Teaching on Call" is the preferred term now, until the 2000s, this was commonly called the "sub-list" and TOC's were known as "substitute teachers"). While Alicia did some TTOCing, in her early years as a teacher, it wasn't something she enjoyed. She recalled one fateful day when it was pouring rain and dark outside. This was before the days of GPS navigation systems and cell phones with Google Maps. She got lost in Maple Ridge and could not find her way back home to Vancouver! Alicia found being a TTOC stressful, so she chose a different career path. In fact, many graduates from teacher education programs do not end up becoming K-12 classroom teachers in public schools. Some teachers go abroad. Others teach in private schools or become school counselors. Some find exciting careers in other industries as the skills attained are easily transferable to other jobs.

## 2    Tutoring Special Needs Students

Alicia dabbled in a number of ventures before she found her niche. For instance, she wrote some ELL textbooks. Also, Alicia continued to explore her arts and crafts. Most importantly, Alicia started her own tutoring business outside her home. With two special needs children of her own, Alicia had to wear several hats – businesswoman, teacher, and parent. She truly became an entrepreneur by circumstance, as her own two boys were not served well by the BC education system, and Alicia had to fill the gap. So, Alicia embarked on her own professional development, taking many courses in inclusive and special education. In order to help her own children and to further her career, Alicia became an expert in autism, attention deficit hyperactivity disorder (ADHD) and teaching children on the spectrum. Gradually, Alicia built up her clientele and gained a reputation as an excellent teacher of special needs children. Alicia was successful in actively engaging a diverse group of children of all ages and abilities. She drew on arts and crafts and her growing *teaching toolkit*, in addition to ongoing and continuous professional development. These are hallmarks of an effective teacher. Alicia found this work challenging but deeply satisfying. She taught a number of children who were on the spectrum, requiring a lot of help but she made a significant difference in the lives of these children and parents appreciated it. Alicia liked helping them. Furthermore, this job suited Alicia's schedule as a mother of two special needs boys (both with ADHD, anxiety and Asperger's). Alicia ran her tutoring business for 15 years. It facilitated a good work-life balance while her two boys were growing up. However, as her business grew, it became more and more challenging to run as she was unable to find qualified help. The one person she hired was unable to do the job, so Alicia had to do it all herself. Because of her desire to help children on the spectrum, Alicia decided to abandon tutoring in order to focus her energies on providing social skills classes to small groups of students, rather than 1:1 tutoring. Schools should be inclusive, but the realities are not so. Alicia has been the strongest advocate for her two boys.

## 3   Teaching Social Skills

Since 2015, Alicia has successfully operated her own business teaching social skills. Alicia has truly found her niche and is filling an important need in her community. Many children have difficulties coping in social situations. School does not work well for these kids. Her own children experienced these challenges. Alicia wanted to help them, and she wanted to help others. Alicia considered doing a master's degree, but the reality is that she is already likely more knowledgeable than many of the instructors. For the most part, Alicia has been self-taught. She has attended numerous workshops, seminars, conferences and has taken special courses. This has involved lots of reading!

Running your own business has some challenges, however. There are financial considerations in becoming an entrepreneur. Students with special needs get some government funding but not all students are eligible. For example, kids on the spectrum, will get government funding but those with ADHD will not. It is sometimes challenging to get paid in a timely manner. It can be frustrating, but it can be very rewarding. Alicia is doing what she loves. She is now integrating art therapy into her lessons. In reflecting on successful lessons, Alicia clearly articulates the joys of teaching:

> Many teachers would say that they did not set out to be teachers, but the teaching "found" them and that has become their passion. I feel quite blessed to be able to do what I do – helping children in need develop and grow.
>
> Teaching small groups and individual students has allowed me to be creative and develop my own resources, often tailored to the child and their challenges. During my practicum, my grade 1 class was learning about dragons and dinosaurs. I made plaster "fossils" for them to dig up and examine, I wrote stories around the theme that incorporated sight words, we cut out dinosaurs from stencils and we all made felt storybook puppets. There were no Educational Assistants (EAs) in that classroom, but there were many children with behavioural and learning challenges

so lots of hands-on support was needed. But I loved it! I remember many of those children fondly, but I also recall how frustrating it was to feel like you couldn't effectively help them all.

The circumstances surrounding my advisor forced me to devise my own employment. This also was something I did not plan, but I was able to adapt, and it allowed me to develop a practice that suited my skills and interests. Through my tutoring services, I was able to now reach individual students and truly help them. One of my first tutoring clients, a very sweet girl, was struggling in school but was most likely undiagnosed on the autism spectrum. I met with her three times a week and helped her with every subject. She was lucky her parents could afford extra help. I saw another disadvantaged student, also struggling in school. I offered this client a reduction in my rates so that their child could have help. Then one day, I turned up and they wouldn't answer their door and hadn't paid for that month's tutoring. It makes me upset that many children that need help, do not receive it. For me, being an entrepreneur, the one down-side is "collecting" which takes away focus from the students and teaching.

Before my practicum, I volunteered with the Learning Disability Association of Vancouver. This experience has truly guided my teaching. Many of these students have had very negative experiences with schools, teachers and learning; in order to engage them, it was important to connect, establish a rapport and insert some fun into the lessons. Making the learning fun and building students' self-esteem has become central to my practice. I created many games for my students; while these games were fun and designed as a break, they also were teaching skills the students needed to focus on. One game we played was "Build a Word" which was designed to help the student sound words out and identify patterns. One of my students delighted in making long, nonsensical words and challenging me to say it; we had a lot of fun with this, and he was still learning the concept. Many of my students expressed how much they looked forward to our sessions; one even said that Monday was her favourite day of the week, because it was tutoring day. Some also told me that I took the time to listen to them and explain things in a way that they understood. This is what it is all about! In contrast, I remember my son's Kindergarten teacher who always met me at the door with a scowl and a story of "what my son did that day." I dreaded pick up time. During parent–teacher night, she drew my artist husband and I over to a wall of chalk pastel art. She pointed out my son's art which was vastly different from the others. It was a direction draw and he had not followed the directions which she saw as defiant and oppositional behaviour. However, upon questioning, my son called it his drawing of 1000 flowers; it was their first time using the chalk pastels and when he opened the box, he couldn't wait to use every single colour. My husband and I saw this as a wonderful expression of creativity, unfortunately she did not agree, and he continued to be misunderstood and labelled as oppositional/defiant. I hope this illustrates the importance of understanding and connecting with students.

With both my sons eventually being diagnosed with Asperger's, ADHD and anxiety, I expanded my learning into different areas. We could not find good social programs, so I set out to create my own based on my research, training and experiences with my boys. I now teach ages 6–22 friendship, communication, executive functioning and social skills; quite ironic, considering how I struggled socially as a child! Teaching this group of learners has been the most rewarding job of my career. I feel that I am really helping those with invisible disabilities that may have otherwise fallen through the cracks. Social emotional learning is perhaps more important than academics but kids on the spectrum do not automatically pick these skills up like most of their peers. The best compliment I ever received doing this work was when an EA enrolled her own child in my classes after observing huge social gains in a student, she worked with in my summer program.

Building my own programs allows me to incorporate materials and techniques from many sources. I have enjoyed using cognitive-behavioural therapy and art therapy strategies to teach social skills and emotional regulation. I love that I can see my students express themselves and connect to others through art, even though they may struggle with verbal output. One of my students joined a free class I was hosting through the BCEdAccess Society.[1] We were making puffy paint and exploring its use. This is a highly sensory art experience, using shaving cream. The joy on his face was evident and his mom sent me some pictures afterwards. Often it was hard for me to discern his emotions, but not this time!

I get so much joy from my work with children, particularly those on the spectrum and the job that I have carved out for myself after initial setbacks, makes me feel like I am truly making a difference in the lives of young people and their parents. I wouldn't change a thing in my teaching career because it has brought me to where I am now.

**Note**

1  See https://bcedaccess.com

CHAPTER 13

# Three Sensei: Novice, Mid-Career & Veteran Teachers

## 1   Narrative of Miss Sakaguchi, Novice Teacher

At the time of this research, back in 2002–2003, Miss Sakaguchi was in her second year of teaching English and her first-year teaching Band at Sakura High School in Tochigi. She is a highly competent and dedicated professional who spends long hours at school devoting most of her energy and free time to her work. Miss Sakaguchi is an outstanding example of young teachers in Japan. Her story while unique captures the atmosphere of Japan's teacher acculturation in a rural setting.

Miss Sakaguchi was born in Yokohama in October 1978 but is a long-time resident of Tochigi. She moved to Tochigi at age seven where she grew up in a mid-sized city of about 83,000 people, living just 15 meters away from the local elementary school. At the age of three, her mother bought an English picture book, which she cherished. From an early age, Miss Sakaguchi showed an interest in English. At five, she began to play the piano. It was obvious that Miss Sakaguchi had a gift in the area of music as she excelled in her piano lessons. Later, she learned that she had perfect pitch and could easily imitate sounds and melodies she heard. This talent carried over to her ability to speak and comprehend English.

In elementary school, Miss Sakaguchi had lots of friends but most of them were boys. This is unusual in Japan where gender segregation is ubiquitous from early on. For a short time, the other girls bullied her. This was likely out of jealousy, as she was one of the top students. While this experience was unpleasant, it made her a stronger person and gave her more self-confidence, as she was able to transcend the immature behaviour of her peers. Moreover, this gave her empathy for others, which in later years would prove invaluable in her teaching. While Miss Sakaguchi doesn't recall any specific teachers or moments of inspiration, she indicated that as a young girl she wanted to be an elementary school teacher. In grade 4 she joined the school band and learned to play the flute.

In junior high school, Miss Sakaguchi continued to excel and was again one of the top students. She was good at all her subjects but enjoyed English and band the most. She continued to play the flute, eventually becoming a club leader of the junior and senior high school orchestra. This is quite an honour and distinction as club leaders are nominated by student members and elected by popular consensus. Miss Sakaguchi liked listening to English pop music and this motivated her to learn more English informally on her own. A critical moment for her at this age was her participation in the annual speech contest. In two years of both junior and senior high school she was chosen as the sole representative of her school in Tochigi's speech contest. The intense preparation for these competitions with the support and guidance of her English teacher and the Assistant English Teacher (AET or ALT) helped to further hone her English communication and natural pronunciation. In high school she continued to develop her English to a much higher level. She credits her hard work and natural ability combined with the support from teachers for her success. These characteristics carry over to her teaching philosophy.

Miss Sakaguchi believes that an effective teacher must have a good understanding of students while providing feedback and positive reinforcement to facilitate learning. She sees teaching as a continuous learning process, but she indicated that it is a talent or gift that some will have, and others will not. This notion of teaching being a natural ability is contrary to the typical Japanese belief that teaching is a craft that has to be learned through practice. However, she indicated that if someone has the essential qualities, effective teaching could be further developed through further study and practice. Miss Sakaguchi believes that her interest and ability in music, in particular her good ear and time spent listening to English pop music as a teenager, helped her to develop her English skills. The intense preparation and daily practice for the speech contest was seminal to her future career as an English teacher. While she admits to wanting to be a junior high school teacher, at this point in time she hadn't thought about which subjects she would teach. However, she noted that teaching "seemed like an easy job" and something she thought she was familiar with as a student.

Another important life event for Miss Sakaguchi was her experience as a participant in an exchange program with the USA. In both junior high and high school, she spent 2 weeks abroad. Her home-stay experiences in Pennsylvania and Indiana as well as her travel around the USA put her English to the test. She quickly learned that her English skills would have to be improved considerably in order for her to communicate effectively with native speakers. Miss Sakaguchi still keeps in touch with the host family from her visit as a high school student at the age of 17. As a result of these experiences abroad, she decided that she would like to live in a foreign country.

After graduation from a prestigious girls' public high school in Tochigi, Miss Sakaguchi attended Sophia University in Tokyo. This is an elite top private institution specializing in English and international affairs with more than half the courses taught in English. The faculty comes from all over the world. This prompted her to travel to San Francisco where she studied for nine months earning credits towards her BA from Sophia University. However, she was more interested in sociology, psychology, and general education rather than teaching English grammar. Her experience as a university student in the USA provided her with an opportunity to pursue greater diversity in courses. This liberal arts education appealed to her since it allowed greater flexibility in course selection than was available in her Japanese university. By age 20 she had decided to become a teacher as she had thoroughly enjoyed her experience teaching at a *juku* (cram school) in Tokyo and tutoring Japanese to foreign students while in San Francisco.

Miss Sakaguchi's brief two-week practicum experience in June of her fourth year was perhaps the most significant formal education event along teaching journey. Her sponsor teacher proved to be highly enthusiastic and full of creativity. While Miss Sakaguchi had to work extremely hard during these two weeks, she credits her sponsor teacher for providing her with inspiration to use a variety of teaching strategies. He was most influential in her teacher induction – significantly more so than her designated mentor teacher in first year or any other teacher in her experience as a beginning teacher.

Miss Sakaguchi cares a great deal about her teaching – placing her job as English and Band teacher at Sakura high above all else. This became evident in conversations with colleagues, but the most significant indicator was her recent choice of career over marriage. Miss Sakaguchi was to be married in December of her second year of teaching but broke off the engagement one-month prior in order to pursue her teaching. Her fiancé, also a Tochigi teacher, ten years her senior had insisted she become a traditional wife (bear children, give up her position at Sakura, move to a school closer to his home in order to take care of the family and household) but she couldn't bear the thought of leaving her teaching job at Sakura. In her first year of teaching this seemed a reasonable prospect but in her second year she became to really appreciate her role and got a great deal of personal satisfaction out of her teaching. In particular, Miss Sakaguchi is proud that she has been credited for bringing the school band back into the spotlight having earned the first gold medal in recent years in the annual Tochigi competition. Sakura has a long-standing tradition of excellence in music that had waned in recent years, due to the lack of interest her predecessor had in instructing the band. If she were to leave Sakura, she wonders what would happen to the band program. Finally, Miss Sakaguchi also enjoys helping the students with the speech contest and those who wish to go on exchanges abroad. In her job she has the chance to help students succeed in the same way her teachers helped her. Perhaps this is the most powerful lesson of all.

## 2  Veteran Teacher, Kimura-Sensei's Mentorship of Shimazaki-Sensei

This brings me to my conversations with two teachers I got to know well through my fieldwork: Kimura-sensei and Shimazaki-sensei. At the time of my doctoral research, Mr. Kimura had 14 years of experience at two different schools while Miss Shimazaki had 6 years' experience at Sakura High School only. While they considered each other *dôryo* (colleagues), there was a clear *sempai/kohai* (senior/junior) relationship as Shimazaki-sensei credits Kimura-sensei as the most important and influential mentor (more so than the officially designated mentor) in her first year of teaching. I spoke with each of them separately on several occasions, culminating with a taped interview with each close to the end of my ethnographic research at Sakura High School.

One of the most significant things observed at Sakura High School were inter-relationships between veteran and novice teachers. This is exemplified in my Journal entry from February 21, 2003:

I spoke with Shimazaki from 10:50–11:45. She is 28 years old with 6 years experience at Sakura High School. She is originally from Tochigi. She did her 2-week practicum at Sanno Girls High School. She described this experience as being a "guest" English teacher. Shimazaki mentioned the big theory and practice divide became evident during this experience. She was critical of her preservice teacher training – "I didn't learn anything relevant to teaching at university." She described her first year of teaching by saying, "I dropped into a whole different world." She indicated the formal training at the Education Center was a lot like university, "I could meet with my friends. It was good but experience is the best teacher." Shimazaki feels that the transition from preservice to in-service teaching is too abrupt. However, she had only 14 hours of classes each week in her first year compared to 18 hours and a homeroom now. She got her first homeroom class in her third year of teaching. She recognizes this stage in her career as an important one that represented a significant milestone that carried with it additional challenges. Shimazaki indicated that once she got her own homeroom class she was "complete" or felt like a "whole teacher" and became very happy and satisfied with her job.

During her first year and beyond, Shimazaki received much help from Kimura-sensei who became a sort of surrogate mentor. Her designated mentor teacher was of little help. He seemed too busy. Kimura helped with everything but she also relied on the other teachers that sat close by in the teachers' room.

She agreed that when she moves to another school once again she will have to rely on the guidance of others in order to learn all the new routines in order to fit into that school's culture and so on.

Kimura-sensei has 14 years of experience at two different high schools in Tochigi. He also had a 2-week practicum and mentioned the importance of *sempai* teachers to his own teacher induction. He shared most of Shimazaki's sentiments about the abrupt transition from university to first year teaching saying, "at first I felt a kind of culture shock." We talked mostly about the nature of *sempai/kohai* and teacher relationships. He feels that teachers are fundamentally colleagues who must function within the framework of *sempai/kohai* relationships. He indicated that in his department these Japanese social structures were rather superficial things like just the way they spoke and their behaviour to one another. However, he said that this could lead to problems in some departments and schools where junior teachers would hesitate to offer their opinions to senior teachers or speak their minds clearly to others. Nevertheless, Shimazaki and Kimura share lessons and ideas freely despite their differences in age and experience. Kimura said that the energy and enthusiasm of younger teachers helps rejuvenate the veterans. He feels inspired by the student teachers he has had. Moreover, experiences with younger colleagues have forced him to question some of his time-honoured traditions… to question the status quo and to reflect on how things could be done differently. This is an important finding, but I suspect that he is not typical in this regard. Kimura indicated that the *sempai/kohai* top-down structure is much more rigid in some departments like PE and in other schools as well.

These conversations helped me to confirm that teachers are in fact colleagues. The term "colleague" better captures the relationships between teachers than the literal translation (*dôryo*). However, *sempai* and *kohai* also figure prominently. Finally, these interviews help me to justify my research methodology. I can't apply a critical ethnographic perspective. Social justice and empowerment of new teachers is not culturally appropriate considering teachers have been socialized from a young age within a *sempai/kohai* culture and a society that functions around what Nakane (1970) calls a vertical organization.

## 3   A Tribute to Hiro-Sensei, a Mid-Career Teacher

Imagine living through a 9.0 magnitude earthquake, a 10-meter tsunami, threat of nuclear radiation and hundreds of terrifying aftershocks. Then, imagine someone so dedicated to work, rather than fleeing to the nearest safe haven, or calling in sick, this individual heads to school because classes are in session and education of young children is the highest priority. This is a true story of what transpired at my son's school in Saitama following the Sendai Earthquake of Friday, March 11, 2011. It is a tribute to Hiro-sensei and other teachers in Japan.

On Monday morning, Hiro-sensei awoke at 4 am and caught the first train from his home in Adachi-ku, Tokyo, heading northwest toward Saitama. However, the Japan Rail (JR) train only went as far as Akabane, Tokyo as train service was severely disrupted after the great earthquake and ongoing tremors. While waiting patiently in a long line of distraught commuters to ask the conductor what to do next, the man in front of Hiro-sensei became furious when he learned there were no further trains beyond Akabane. However, Hiro-sensei kept calm. He waited in another long line and boarded a bus bound for Kawaguchi, on the other side of the river. Hours later, he arrived at Kawaguchi, Saitama. Then he set out on the long journey that lay ahead on foot. Hiro-sensei walked an arduous 18 km from Kawaguchi to our elementary school in Omiya. It took over 3 hours! Hiro-sensei finally arrived at school around 11:40 and went straight to the gym to join his colleagues who had been supervising his students since 8:30 am. All grade 6 students were busy preparing for next week's graduation ceremony.

As a result of the threat of nuclear radiation and scientists' ominous prediction of a greater than 70% chance of a 7.0 magnitude earthquake, school officials dismissed children early Monday and declared Tuesday a school holiday. Wednesday through Friday were half-days at school as a result of scheduled rotating 3-hour blackouts. Hiro-sensei decided to stay overnight at the school rather than attempt to return home. He joined the principal, vice-principal, and other teachers in the gym for a round-the-clock vigil. In the event of emergency evacuations, it is the responsibility of administrators to remain at school, as a safety mechanism to help the community. Teachers often share this burden and other significant administrative duties. Another example of the incredible dedication and sense of duty teachers exemplify can be found in the story of a teacher I know who lives just 25 km from the Fukushima nuclear plant. While government officials ordered the evacuation of all residents within a 20 km radius and told others within a 30 km radius to remain indoors, this woman and other teachers in the vicinity continued to teach and carry on other extended duties in spite of the personal health risk to themselves and their families.

During the week following the disaster in Japan, many people chose to stay indoors or to flee the Kanto area all together. Those that remained lined up to fill their cars with gas and stock up on essentials. The panic-ridden public feared the worst, in the wake of earthquakes, tsunamis and threat of nuclear fallout – a tragedy described by the PM as "the biggest challenge facing Japan since WWII." Foreigners were told to leave the country. Worried housewives donned masks and covered themselves from head to foot as they ventured outside to brave the frenzied crowds to buy batteries, emergency gear, food and other essentials. Meanwhile, people in the Tohoku region were coping with the aftermath of a major catastrophe. Lack of food, water, adequate shelter and communication with loved ones continued to test the strength and determination of survivors in Sendai, Fukushima and other areas hardest hit.

Tokyoites had different challenges to face, however – train service continued to be troublesome throughout the week with severe disruptions; convenience stores were closed at odd hours; and shelves were stripped bare. People were stressed. The situation appeared increasingly grim as the national NHK news reports and video clips circulated, highlighting the massive devastation and aftermath of the disaster unfolding.

Despite all this, my son's teacher continued to do his duties to his utmost. It is unbelievable that this teacher would travel such a great distance on foot to reach the school and then chose to stay there rather than retreat to the comfort of home. Nevertheless, I'm convinced that many teachers would have done exactly the same thing because they care deeply for their students. It is time the public recognized the enduring efforts of teachers, their professionalism and dedication. In these difficult times, please do not forget to acknowledge the amazing work done by teachers.

## 4  Teacher Relationships

Teachers must care deeply for children. It is all about nurturing caring, trusting, relationships and creating lasting bonds through *kizuna* (bonds), *kankei* (inter-relationships) and *kizuki* (with-it-ness). In the words of a first-year teacher in my doctoral research, it means

> [T]o trust each other [teachers/students/others] and to do things for each other and the class as a whol… Children are dear to us. If other teachers compliment or praise my students it makes me happy. (Conversation with Sachie and four other novice teachers January 28, 2003)

My research into Japan's teacher acculturation has enabled me to identify a number of key features that I believe are essential elements to effective teaching (Howe, 2005a, 2005b, 2017). In particular, the following attributes are noteworthy: strength of relationships, collegiality, collaboration, mentoring, and emphasis on the peer group. In addition, lesson study and communities of learning are seminal to the success of Japanese education. Narrative pedagogies relate to many Japanese cultural practices including *kankei*, *kizuna*, and *kizuki*. These are important, integral and tacit elements of Japanese teachers' practices because they embody mind and heart. Japanese society values *kankei* and access to networks of trusted people (Howe & Arimoto, 2014). The significant bonds or *kizuna* formed between teachers and students and amongst peers in Japan is noteworthy. I experienced this phenomenon of *kizuna* with my teacher education students during my decade in Japanese higher education. Finally, the concept of *kizuki* or with-it-ness is something that is difficult to define but most teachers can identify this important tacit classroom skill in observations of other teachers. This is something it takes years to obtain but through the practice of lesson study it is readily observed, learned, practiced, and mastered.

Extended time in a foreign culture has given me a profound understanding of what it means to be treated as an Other (see Howe & Xu, 2013). This in turn has fostered transcultural teaching and empathy for others. This is very important given Canada's immigration policies attracting more and more international students, forming increasingly larger proportions of our Canadian classrooms. Furthermore, my experience outside my own culture has helped me to see the significance of *kankei*, *kizuna*, and *kizuki* as these Japanese teacher qualities all involve placing other people's needs before one's own. These are essential skills for global citizens of the 21st century. I believe these practices combined with narrative pedagogies, show great promise in providing much needed empathy for others within our ever more interconnected world.

CHAPTER 14

# Mari and Ken: Japan's Next Generation of Teachers

## 1   Marathons and High-Stakes Testing in Japan

It is not whether you win or lose but how you play the game… but not within Japanese schooling, rife with high stakes testing and marathon races from an early age… (Howe & Arimoto, 2014).

Many years ago, my eldest son ran a marathon at his local elementary school in Saitama, where we used to live. He received a congratulatory "certificate of achievement" noting his participation and 79th place. He came to dread this annual ritual. It damaged his fragile self-esteem and emerging identity by blatantly focusing on his physical condition. While students cheered him on at the finish line, inside he was hurting.

Many of my former university students in Japan have shared in this humiliation – one indicated the marathon was her worst memory of kindergarten! While proponents argue it builds character and is a motivator for improving physical fitness, most educators agree such methods are questionable in their efficacy and effectiveness. Thus, I hope teachers and parents in Japan, will lobby to abandon this practice.

Nevertheless, school marathons continue throughout Japan and are a longstanding tradition. They won't disappear without controversy. Like *undokai* (sports day), it takes on Olympic proportions, involving the entire school and is widely attended by parents wielding their video cameras, cheering their children on to "victory." However, unlike *undokai*, the focus appears to be on winning, rather than participation and physical fitness.

On the other hand, the Japanese school system places so much emphasis on 'equality' and uniformity there is little room for individuality. Athletic students must have some source of pride and accomplishment. Moreover, all children must eventually confront and overcome their weaknesses by finding their self-esteem in something they can excel in. It is up to teachers and parents to provide love and support to give children the strength to get them through the tough times, and instill a sense of pride, self-confidence and self-worth by recognizing and acknowledging what they are good at.

What is the purpose of the marathon in Japanese schooling? According to the Ministry of Education, Sports and Culture (MEXT), policy goals of physical education include achieving a society that is active in sports throughout life by giving everybody the opportunity to engage in sport anywhere, anytime and forever, regardless of physical strength, age, capability, interest and purpose. But the marathon doesn't achieve these goals. Rather, it further alienates the physically challenged or average students, while glorifying the few winners. Why rank students? Wouldn't it be much better to have students run in heats with others of similar qualifying times? Then individuals could compete against themselves and aim to improve their personal best.

Are public displays of ranking of students done in other subjects? Imagine an English essay competition where all students are ranked and those ranks clearly posted. My bi-lingual and highly literate son would have easily come first – others wouldn't stand a chance… That is unethical and unfair you say! Well, it is analogous to the marathon race. Furthermore, this is also painfully similar to the race to enter the best universities, the ranking of institutions and applicants, and the posting of entrance exam results in Japan.

Throughout the world, there is a perceived crisis of "falling behind" as international achievement tests become standardized measures of success. Teachers are increasingly under pressure to cover 'core' content at the expense of arts, humanities, global citizenship education and social issues like climate change. Teaching to the test is becoming more common at all grade levels. But teachers should look beyond the curriculum to gain a broader international perspective and to achieve a deeper cross-cultural understanding of our niche within the global village.

Finally, wealthy parents send their children to the best *juku* (cram schools) from an early age giving their children an unprecedented edge. The super elites literally buy a spot for their children into the best universities, bypassing university entrance exams. The Japanese education system is in effect helping to reproduce socioeconomic inequities. But isn't Japan supposedly a meritocratic country built on social mobility and principles of equality? Unfortunately, high stakes testing and marathons perpetuate the class discrepancies and systemic inequalities within Japanese society. It's time to change these traditions. Who is up to the challenge of educational reform? I believe there is a growing cohort of progressive-minded transcultural teachers in Japan. For two such examples, please read Mari and Ken-sensei's stories that follow.

## 2    Mari-Sensei's Transcultural Journey

Mari first studied math in university. She graduated in 2004. Then she taught high school math in Chiba (near Tokyo) before joining the Japan International Cooperation Agency (JICA) in order to volunteer as an overseas teacher in

Africa. In a bold move, she quit her job as a high school math teacher, to teach in Uganda as a volunteer with JICA. Mari spent nearly 2½ years in Uganda. Upon returning to Japan, Mari wondered how she could build on her teaching background and extensive cross-cultural experience. She wanted to find a way to incorporate her experiences with her teaching. This prompted her to go back to university to become an English teacher. After spending time abroad, Mari decided to go back to school, specifically to become an English teacher. One of the main reasons, Mari returned to school to study English was to enable her to integrate her life-changing experiences in her teaching. While living in Uganda, Mari gained a sense of all the things Japanese people take for granted… things such as clean drinking water, and adequate supplies of basic necessities like food and shelter. Moreover, Mari came to better understand Japanese culture and her own self. Finally, she came to critically question gender differences prevalent in both African societies and Japanese society. Mari also came to appreciate the importance of early childhood education, literacy, and education for all. She felt teaching English was the best way she could integrate her cross-cultural experiences with teaching for global citizenship in a curriculum that is strictly adhered to.

Mari was one of my most interesting students in my composition class and oral communication classes of 2008. In these classes she had the opportunity to reflect on her various transcultural experiences and to share them with her classmates. In the oral communication class, she gave a moving presentation of her experience living abroad and teaching children in Uganda. In the writing class she wrote in a journal and she wrote a paper entitled, "The challenges of students: The case of Uganda." In her essay she writes:

> Uganda is known as one of the developing countries in Africa. Life expectancy is [only] 46 years old. The literacy rate is 72.6% – that is 147 among 192 countries. I stayed there for 2 years and 5 months. During my days, I asked many questions to my colleagues and my students. I also joined programs, which enhance teaching schools and exchanged opinions with teachers from other schools… It is important for readers to know the education problems for developing countries… Education is very important to people. School is not the only place where people study but also get wisdom or knowledge for survival. (Mari, research paper abstract, submitted January 2008)

Mari was given the chance to reflect on her transborder experience in Uganda in various classroom settings and ways. In the composition class, she wrote in her journal and it became a catalyst for her research paper. I also invited her to share her experiences through multi-media presentations to her classmates in other classes. Mari shared a JICA video and prepared a moving Power Point presentation with her own photos and text. She was happy to be able to teach others about the struggles of people in Uganda and about significant lessons in gender equity that are just as applicable to women in Japan as they are in Uganda. Students' transborder experiences have the potential to change the curriculum, teaching and learning of others. Travel abroad for personal and professional growth is becoming an integral part of experience and education for an increasing number of students in teacher education programs. However, it isn't yet an official policy in Japan and the spaces for exchange students are rather limited. It is left up to students to make their own arrangements. This could be improved with reforms to teacher education programs to include a component of comparative and international education. As MEXT has proposed changing the teacher education programs to a post-degree 2-year master's, there could be the provision for more transcultural education. I look forward to that prospect, but it is many years if and when it becomes a reality.

Unfortunately, Mari was unable to obtain a job teaching English as she had hoped. Mari became a math teacher at a private high school in Tochigi, north of Tokyo. She indicated that she would like to use her extensive transcultural experiences in her teaching. However, at the time of this research, she said that it would be difficult to integrate her experiences into the math curriculum but possible in homeroom class. As this was Mari's first year to have a homeroom class, she was excited about this new teaching responsibility and opportunity.

Mari is happy teaching math, however she indicated she'd still like to teach English. After all, that was why she went back to school in the first place. In addition to Uganda, she has traveled to Tanzania, Rwanda and Vietnam. Mari indicated these international cross-cultural experiences are by far the most significant critical events, shaping her personal, practical and professional knowledge. Mari's experience in Uganda has had a profound effect on Mari's teaching philosophy. One interesting point is that Mari indicated that there is a problem with English teachers who have a fear of talking to the Assistant Language Teacher (ALT). It appears that many of the senior English teachers at this prestigious private high school continue to do things the traditional ways. This became evident in my conversation with another former student who happens to be teaching with Mari. He is teaching English. Both Ken and Mari came to my office in May of 2012 to have a *teacher-to-teacher conversation* with me. It was nice catching up with them. Both are now married and have several years of teaching under their belts. They are no longer struggling novice teachers but are well on their way to becoming confident, experienced professionals.

Nevertheless, as younger teachers they still face challenges. Next let me tell you Ken's story.

## 3  Ken-Sensei's Struggle against the Status Quo

Ken was born in Chicago and lived there for two years before returning to Japan as a youngster. This brief period during his formative years gave Ken an ear for English. He was among the most promising students of his cohort. I taught him from 2006–2010 and thus became very familiar with him. Ken had excellent pronunciation and a good ear. He was a natural. Ken scored nearly 100% on my listening tests in first year… almost unheard of! Ken took a number of courses with me including communication courses in first year, a writing course in second year, and a seminar in third year. The seminar allows students to reflect on social issues and to give a presentation on a topic relating to global citizenship education. I recall one striking incident where Ken made a profound comment during a seminar. After one of Ken's peers made a presentation on street children in the Philippines, the students were asked, "Has your impression of street kids changed as a result of my presentation?" Ken's response was something like

> Thank you for your presentation. Yes, my attitude and opinion has radically changed. I used to think street kids were someone else's problem, but now I see that we as a society need to care for our children. We need to help others who are in need. These children are on the streets for various reasons and not because they are delinquents or misfits.

The general consensus among this group of students was they agreed with Ken's reflection.

Since graduation in 2010, Ken has been teaching English to junior and senior high school students at the same private high school as Mari. He enjoys his job and has survived the critical period of the first three years. But his first few years weren't easy. Ken recalls that there was a huge difference between the carefree life of a student and the responsibilities of teaching. In addition, he is now married. So, it is no exaggeration to say that Ken's life has changed significantly since I knew him as a student.

Ken laments that all his senior colleagues still use grammar translation methods of teaching English. These teachers still teach English without using it in any practical way. Most of the English teachers at this elite private school are still embarrassed to talk with foreigners – including the ALT working at the school! Ken prefers a more communicative approach, but he has to be careful what he says and does in order not to upset his senior colleagues. Ken is among the youngest of the teachers at his school. He is keenly aware of his place in the teaching hierarchy. Unfortunately, shortly after our conversation, Ken told me that he quit teaching due to pervasive resistance from his seniors. He became disillusioned and frustrated as he was unable to implement global citizenship education and transformative teaching pedagogies within the rigid Japanese school system.

CHAPTER 15

# Carolyn: Sixties Scoop Story of Indigenous Resilience

## 1    The Importance of Family and Community

My biological mother was nineteen years old when she gave birth to me in the late 1960s. Before getting the chance to even hold me, nurses took me away from her and I became part of the now infamous "Sixties Scoop."

Landing on the heels of the Indian Residential Schools, the Sixties Scoop was an extension of existing paternalistic policies in Canada that sought the assimilation of Indigenous cultures and communities. It was a large-scale removal or "scooping" Indigenous babies and children from their Indigenous families and communities, to be adopted out to predominantly non-Indigenous middle-class families both inside and outside Canada from 1951 to the mid-1980s. Research shows more than 20,000 Indigenous children were removed from their families and communities with the largest number removed during the decade of the 1960s (Sinclair & Dainard, 2020).

I was raised in a small northern pulp and paper mill town. My adoptive father was of English descent and my adoptive mother was half English and half Cree. I believe the half Cree part of my adoptive mom helped me cope during my childhood as she was authentically Indigenous in many ways. She understood Indigenous ways of knowing and being and helped me feel connected, safe, loved, and understood which was very important as most Sixties Scoop survivors feel disconnected from their lives.

My mother believes weaving love and belonging throughout everything we do with our children is a natural element of child-rearing. This includes truly listening to your children's voice and allowing them the agency they need to learn and grow. She listened to my ideas, encouraged me to try new things and let me make mistakes. She would ask me "so, how did that go?" and we would discuss it. Our talks always ended with hugs, and if we were on the couch, she would lie down and make room for me too. I recall having moments like this in high school when we struggled to both fit on the couch because I was too big, but she never said no. Most adults I encountered as a young person believed children and youth should be seen and not heard. I felt de-valued by that and over time began to internalize the message that my voice did not matter. My mother's beliefs and values countered this but was small in scope in comparison to the many others.

She believes in the power of community and how we all play a role in raising children to live their lives in a good way by helping others, giving back to community, and by prioritizing healthy relationships. She taught me to respect the land as it provides for us with meat, berries, and fertile soil to grow food. We lived ten miles out of town on one and a half acres and had a very large vegetable garden. Although I enjoyed our vegetables and rhubarb etc., I really disliked all the weeding I had to do! She was always thankful for how much our garden produced, and when we had a good season of berry picking, mostly saskatoons. Many summer evenings and weekends during berry picking season were spent with a jug of juice (beer for my dad), sandwiches and emptied out Napoleon ice cream buckets for the berries. My whole family would pile into the car and off we would go to pick berries. Her saskatoon jam, jelly and pies were the best and she would often gift them to others in our community.

We also had plenty of bannock. My mother is Swampy Cree from southern Saskatchewan, so the bannock she was taught to make was baked in the oven, not deep-fried like it is commonly experienced. My mom and her family are all well-versed in bannock, even though it is not a traditional Indigenous food (Scottish in origin) it has been adopted as an Indigenous food and we love it! Reflecting on this now, I realize that my mom never shared bannock with the community.

My father was not a fisherman, but my mother believes in the importance of fish as part of our diet. I think it's 'blood memory' as fish have been an important staple of the First Nations diet since time immemorial. My mom, however, also did not fish, so she managed to connect with another First Nations man from the area (somehow) who would fish for us and drop off the 'seasonal catch' to our doorstep in a big, black plastic bag. Sometimes she would pay him, sometimes she would trade for it, then my mother and father would spend the next week gutting, filleting, and either smoking and/or canning it. They tried to get me to help, but I hated both the taste and smell of fish so spent that week each year playing outside until I was told to come back in at dinnertime. I still do not like fish and my family good-heartedly tease me about not being "a very good Indian."

My mother and her siblings also spoke some Cree language. Her mother, my grandmother, was fluent in both Cree and English but only English was fluently passed on to my mother and her siblings by design. It was dangerous in Canada in the 1930s to be First Nations for many reasons, Residential Schools being one, so they chose not to pass on the Cree language. Some words slipped through though, as they do, and I was exposed to a little bit of Cree growing up. I recall the word astum (come here), tansi (hello) and hihi (thank you). Along with bannock, I knew at a young age such First Nations cultural elements should remain within the walls of our house to not draw too much attention.

Indigenous ways of knowing and being significantly contrast European ways of knowing and being. When you remove an Indigenous child from their Indigenous family and community, they are still Indigenous in ways that cannot be erased. I am First Nations from the Coast Salishan cultural group and my adoptive mother is half Cree. Although all First Nations have different perspectives and worldviews, there are common elements that are reflected in most, if not all, First Nations. One of many is that we see the world through a holistic lens, and another is that we share a darker skin colour. These two elements strongly differentiated me from those around me in the community where I grew up.

Being brown in a school and community that was predominately white created barriers to my success. During the 1970s and 1980s First Nations people were often viewed as 'lazy, drunk Indians' and inferior to mainstream white society. Such bias caused many First Nations youth when going to school or living in a white community to try to look and act white as an attempt to fit in better. I've heard stories of Indigenous youth covering up their skin in the summer to prevent tanning and dying their hair blonde. At one point as a young person, I learned Spanish to distract people from thinking I was First Nations, anything to separate myself from the existing stereotypes. Having darker skin caused erroneous assumptions by the white community which have been reflected in dialogue with other First Nations from this era. They talk about how they were often overlooked, dismissed, and sometimes treated abusively, all of which I experienced as well.

One of the ways in which my history as being a Sixties Scoop survivor has impacted me is my struggle with identity issues and not feeling like I truly belong anywhere. It's called "being lost between two worlds" and it refers to how First Nations do not fit well into white society, but also do not fit well into Indigenous society. Many Sixties Scoop survivors have not been welcomed back into their home nations when they try to reconnect because they are considered outsiders, and in most cases, they were. For example, I know very little about my nation, its customs, protocols, and cultural structures. The policy of the Sixties Scoop has impacted and continues to impact Indigenous peoples and by extension, all Canadians as we collectively come to terms with past decisions and engage with the process of reconciliation.

## 2   Reflections on Indigenizing Our Pedagogies of Practice

I became a teacher in my thirties after I married and had a child. There are pivotal moments in your life when something happens that has the capacity to change your perspective. Having a child was the greatest and most influential event of my life and influenced my decision to become a teacher. A lesser event, but one of significance was while I was in university and was introduced to patterns of learning. Patterns of learning are when you look at ways that societies learn best. Learning styles can be described as typical and preferred ways of perceiving, thinking, solving problems, drawing inferences, and remembering. At a societal level, and over several generations, patterns of learning are taught – experienced – practiced, then passed on genetically, which can make adaptation to other styles of learning quite challenging. Although you cannot say specific patterns of learning are true for every member of a society, they suit most individuals of the same group. It also takes multiple generations for individuals to unlearn these patterns.

At this event I learned First Nations patterns of learning are quite specific as they are intuitive, oral, imaginal, and learned best through the process of observation, reflection, hands-on experience, and cooperative work. First Nations worldviews and perspectives are holistic with a focus on the connectedness of everything (Pewewardy, 2002). This is in direct contrast to English patterns of learning the Canadian education system was modelled on, where learning is individual, written, analytical, and often taught in the abstract. Eurocentric in nature, they also focus on the small parts as opposed to the whole.

My learning style fits how First Nations learn best. Due to the conflict in learning styles and no accommodations made from the education system to meet my specific learning needs, I performed poorly in school. I felt disconnected from the curriculum and struggled to keep up in most subjects, always believing I was not very smart. Understanding societal patterns of learning allowed me to see that the problem was system-related and not a reflection of my learning capabilities. This was pivotal because I had always bought into the 'Indigenous peoples are inferior' narrative I had been fed my whole life, and I thought being unsuccessful in school was proof. Understanding patterns of learning provided the opportunity to feel more self-confident and allowed space for a different version of the story to emerge. I considered how my negative experience in education could empower me to create positive educational experiences for future First Nations students.

As someone who has experienced what it feels like to often be overlooked, easily dismissed and unheard, I ensure my students do not experience this in my classroom and really push them to find their own voice and agency with their choices. Building positive relationships with students is essential in understanding their behaviour and, subsequently, helping in their learning. When mutual trust is established, one is better able to understand individual student needs, academic and social barriers, and ways in which they learn best. Understanding commonalities among students who share cultural worldviews and perspectives, as well as challenges, also aids in how to best approach and adapt learning strategies to specific group needs that will motivate instead of de-motivate. Doing so falls under the term equitable pedagogy, an approach that has been close to my heart since deciding to become a teacher.

Ironically, however, when first becoming a teacher, I promptly landed into the familiar Eurocentric style of teaching that I reflect upon now as another pivotal moment. I introduced a family tree project to my mostly Indigenous group of primary students. They were to add one leaf to their tree to represent each one of their family members beginning with grandparents, or great grandparents, parents, aunts, uncles, cousins, then them along with their siblings. It was supposed to be a quick and fun activity. I thought I had made plenty of leaves for them to apply to their trees, but as the afternoon went on, they just kept adding more and more leaves and I ran out. When I went around the room to investigate why, I saw that they had added leaves to represent their aunties, uncles, cousins and many sisters and brothers and I realized what I had not anticipated. First Nations kinship is different than European kinship systems. Family for First Nations is relationship-based, not blood-related based, so one person may have many, many, aunties for example as well as sisters and brothers. The concept of cousins is not First Nations as they are considered siblings. Whether I was upset because the activity was taking too long, or that I had to make more leaves, I don't recall, but I do distinctly remember advising them that family meant only blood-related relatives. They informed me I was wrong about that, and we engaged in a quick power struggle before I reneged my position and began cutting out more leaves. In the end, I cut out leaves for days until their trees could hold no more. They were beautiful and the students were so very proud of them!

Disrupting colonial educational structures by infusing Indigenous ways of knowing and being changes students' understanding of the world by broadening their vistas and cultivating independent thought. Looking at the world through alternate perspectives allows them to reflect upon their own identities and see how they fit into the world around them. This reformation becomes a part of their own story to carry forward with them.

When educators follow a framework that challenges established systems of belief that support Eurocentric practices that have silenced other ways of knowing and being, all students benefit. Addressing the needs of the individual along with considering the collective and the community allows learners to see themselves reflected in the spaces they learn thereby creating a more inclusive and positive experience.

My first twelve years of teaching have been a succession of emancipatory experiences as I moved further and further away from the negative memories of my own grade school experience. When I think about the Truth and Reconciliation Commission's 94 Calls to Action (2015), I think about the opportunities Canadians have, especially educators, to ensure past wrongs such as Residential Schools and the Sixties Scoop, are never repeated. I also consider how the Calls to Action give us the chance to collectively participate in creating a better Canada to leave behind to our children and our children's children. To me, reconciliation means reconciling our past by being a part of a future with benefits that extend far beyond ourselves out to our community and to our nation. It is the re-building of healthy relationships that Canada was originally built upon and the belief system my Cree mother instilled in me. We are walking "in a good way." Hihi (thank you).

### Acknowledgement

Carolyn Anderson is a TRU sessional instructor and SD73 District Coordinator of Aboriginal Education. The author wishes to thank Carolyn for this chapter which is entirely in her own words.

CHAPTER 16

# Marie: Secwépemc Language Teacher

Thompson Rivers University campuses are on the traditional lands of the Tk'emlúps te Secwépemc (Kamloops campus) and the T'exelc (Williams Lake campus) within Secwépemc'ulucw, the traditional and unceded territory of the Secwépemc. The region TRU serves also extends into the territories of the St'át'imc, Nlaka'pamux, Tŝilhqot'in, Nuxalk, and Dakelh.

## 1   Background

*Marie Sandy ren skwekwst. Te T̓éxelc re st̓ʾé7kwen, k̓émell ne T̓kemlúps re múmtwen. Len kikyé7e, Anastasia ell Elizabeth le skweskwest.s. Well len xpé7e, Frank, Olaf, ell Norman le skweskwest.s. Ren kí7ce, Helen re skwest.s. Ren qe7tse, Michael re skwest.s. W7ec re é7elkstwen, ne Thompson Rivers University, ell School District 73.*

Marie was born and raised in Williams Lake, British Columbia within *Secwépemcelúcw*, the traditional and unceded territory of the *Secwépemc*. She is the second daughter of Michael Grimsrud and Helen Sandy. Marie has a younger sister that also became a teacher, who now lives in Australia. Marie's older sister was raised by her maternal grandmother who felt strongly about the importance of education. As a child, Marie was read to daily. Literacy was deemed very important. Schooling was something that flowed well from her rich home learning environment. Marie was fortunate to have supportive family. In addition, Marie had some highly influential teachers. Marie fondly remembers her grade 3 teacher who created a comfortable and safe classroom. Both Marie's parents encouraged her to pursue higher learning. At age six, in 1987, Marie attended her auntie's convocation at the University of British Columbia (UBC, Vancouver campus). Two years later Marie's auntie passed the bar and became a practicing lawyer. This is noteworthy for First Nations peoples as higher education was, at that time, a major accomplishment. Most importantly, it left a lasting impression on Marie. From a young age it was assumed she would go to university.

Marie was an average student in elementary school. But she "hung out with all the smart kids" in high school, which had a positive impact, helping Marie to aspire to study more to get into university. Marie in turn inspired her cousin who was her best friend to go to university. That friend is currently working towards her PhD in Land Use Planning at the University of Northern British Columbia.

In reflecting on her first year of university, Marie mused, "I wasn't sure what I wanted to do yet…" Nevertheless, Marie took courses that interested her – history, archaeology, and psychology. She did not plan to become a teacher. With the generous assistance of funding from her band, Marie completed her first degree from Thompson Rivers University (TRU) in 2005. "It felt a bit anti-climactic," said Marie. Upon graduation, Marie worked briefly in the health sector. She also worked in the band office. But she did not feel challenged in these jobs. Something was missing. Then, she worked with the Secwépemc Cultural Education Society (SCES) as a Language Technician. She assisted Mona Jules and worked closely with her. Mona Jules is widely known as a leader in the field, and one of the strongest advocates for Secwépemc language and culture. That was where Marie realized this was a way she could contribute and help the language revitalization movement. It was at this time, that Marie started to think about becoming a teacher. While Marie took Secwépemc language classes in high school, she felt that the course material was repetitive due to language teacher turnover, and their lack of formal teacher training. The classes she took with the Secwépemc Cultural Education Society (SCES) however were great. They inspired her to think "Hey… I can do this… Teaching and being a language teacher is a possibility!"

Next, in 2006, Marie moved back to Williams Lake and began working as a receptionist for the band office. Soon thereafter, she became aware of a new internship program within the BC Ministry, called the Aboriginal Youth Internship Program (now called the Indigenous Youth Internship Program), to work in combination with a Provincial Ministry, and an Indigenous organization. So, in 2007, she was part of the first year of this exciting new program. Marie worked within the Ministry of Advanced Education Skills and Training (AEST), in Victoria for 9 months, and then with the Tsilhqotin National Government for 3 months. It gave her a window into other First Nations organizations. It was a great exposure to the world of education. This was a critical incident that led to her decision to go into teaching. In this job, she learned the importance of lifelong learning. Moreover, Marie came to realize that learning happens after university. Marie worked with a key FNESC (First Nations Education Steering Committee) founder, Christa Williams who was a mentor and encouraged her. However, this was in the midst of the 2008–2009 economic downturn, so she moved back home.

Kamloops has always felt like home to Marie. She soon got a job with *Tk'emlúps te Secwépemc* as a researcher, and then went onto work with the Kamloops School District (SD73) as an Aboriginal Education Worker. Also, it was at this time, she met her life-partner. Lots of positive things were happening in Marie's life. It was a time of renewal and change. As an Aboriginal Education Worker, she got some great experience, working in an elementary school. In this role, she connected with students, faculty and staff. Marie got invitations to help classroom teachers with cultural lessons. Her knowledge was starting to be utilized a lot more. Marie's self-confidence was growing – She was teaching!

One lesson, Marie fondly recalls was where she would introduce young students to the different seasons. The best activity was bringing in some traditional plants into the classroom that she knew grew on the school grounds, giving them their uses, whether that be medicinal, technical or for sustenance. Marie would then take students outside and do a scavenger hunt with them, also pointing out the sustainable and safety harvesting practices. That was when Marie realized she had worldly knowledge and a teaching niche. So, Marie applied to the TRU Bachelor of Education (BEd) Elementary Program in 2016. Marie did a similar impromptu ethnobotany walk and lesson with her fellow TRU teacher candidates during her first week of classes. It was a memorable experience for all (including her teacher, the author of this book)! Because she had already received funding from the band for her first degree, she had to cobble together money/scholarships/funding for the BEd program. Thankfully, she was able to attend and graduated in 2018. Marie really enjoyed the BEd program. She did her long practicum in her hometown of Williams Lake, which was awesome. She taught grade 3 and had a great experience. Highlights from her early teaching included drumming for students. Marie started and ended each day with songs.

Marie mentioned storytelling and a lesson in her practicum, inspired by one of her professors at TRU. Once she started teaching full days on the long practicum… This was when she felt "I am a teacher now!" She was so tired after work, that she needed a ½ hour nap after school, before driving home! It was really interesting working with different students, schools, and grades but it was exhausting. So, after a few months, Marie chose to focus on teacher teaching on call (TTOC) work in Kamloops. Marie provided the following advice for prospective TTOCs: "It is important to be up front with students and body breaks are important!"

Marie is a TTOC in SD73 (she has a few months experience in Merritt and nearly 3 years in SD73) and works as a sessional at TRU now. At the time of this writing, she is also completing her MEd and is currently working on her thesis. As most novice teachers will agree, it is not easy being a TTOC. Going into another teacher's classroom can be very challenging. So, Marie was very nervous at the start of her TTOC work. She was worried. But she found it a valuable learning experience. During this formative time, Marie kept a journal.

(See Appendix B for Marie's insightful Journal entries from TTOC work in Merritt and Kamloops and her TRU Secwépemc Language Teaching.) Reflective journal writing helped Marie to make sense of her experiences as a novice teacher. It is highly recommended that teachers keep a journal. It is not necessary to keep detailed accounts of your lessons, nor should a journal replace lesson plans. But a journal can be very helpful. Marie's journal may serve as an example for others to follow. Marie also found it helpful to reflect back on her educational philosophy. The core values she articulated as a student still remain true to this day.

## 2 Educational Philosophy

### 2.1 *Indigenous Knowledge/Ways of Knowing*

I come from a line of strong women knowledge keepers: my mother the storyteller/steward of the land, Túme Jeannie the linguist/steward of the land/nurse/school counsellor, Aunty Nancy the law keeper/lawyer, and Túme Amy the steward of the land/linguist/social worker. These women have shaped my educational philosophy. They are all knowledge keepers in my family, and they have each passed me portions of my Secwépemc heritage knowledge. Family and community are an important part of identity. Students need to know who they are, which influences the way they see the world. I identify strongly with the First Peoples Principles of Learning. I strongly believe that you can learn just as much out on the land as you can in a classroom. As an Indigenous person, I have grown up with a strong sense of stewardship of the land. My family members made sure that we were brought onto the land to see what we are protecting for the next generation. My aunts brought me berry picking, gathering traditional medicines and foods; my uncles brought me hunting and fishing, and my cousin took me trapping. I learned just as much on these excursions onto the land, as I did in a classroom. Where do the best berries grow? If the deer count is down this year, how many can we take this season to ensure that the next generation will still have deer? The sun and the wind are great ways to cure salmon. How does this happen? Do medicines grow better on the sunny side or shady side of the mountain? These are all questions that had gone through my mind whilst walking the land with my family members.

> Indigenous knowledge comprises all knowledge pertaining to a particular people and its territory, the nature or use of which has been transmitted from generation to generation. (Battiste, 2002, p. 8)

> Indigenous knowledge comprises the complex set of technologies developed and sustained by Indigenous civilizations. Often oral and symbolic, it is transmitted through the structure of Indigenous language and passed on to the next generation through modelling, practice, and animation, rather than through the written word. (Battiste, 2002, p. 2)

> Indigenous teachings provide that every child, whether Aboriginal or not, is unique in his or her learning capacities, learning styles, and knowledge bases. (Battiste, 2002, p. 15)

### 2.2   *Montessori*

I was highly influenced by the Montessori pedagogy during our recent field trip to Aberdeen Elementary School. I had been unprepared for the experience of touring the six Montessori classrooms, but I was definitely intrigued. I had not known much about Montessori schooling. I did not know that there are usually three grades within a classroom and that the students work at their own pace and within their areas of interest. Moreover, I discovered that their learning takes place with hands-on materials and that the classroom would be set up so open and with centres of subjects (i.e., math area, science area, art area).

### 2.3   *Progressivism*

As an Aboriginal Education Worker for SD73, I was able to see different teaching styles within classrooms, and I began to admire the teachers in my school. In the 2014/2015 school year I participated in professional development days on the BC Ed Plan's new curriculum. I began to see the benefit of an inquiry-based learning style for our students. This introduction of the new curriculum influenced my developing pedagogy. I identified with inquiry-based learning that can take part over a few lessons during a week or span a school year. Encountering Dewey and Kilpatrick with their ideas of student-based learning (although Dewey had leaned more towards a teacher modelled, but student-based learning) helped define the educational theory with which I identified.

In conclusion, I still identify strongly with my Indigenous Ways of Knowing, but I have identified with two other theories that I believe dovetail nicely into my own personal educational philosophy.

> Montessori education is organized to the core… Children are calmly working alone or in groups. And their work is organized. They are concentrating, carrying out activities in a series of steps that have been shown to them by the teacher or other children. (Lillard, 2005, p. 21)

Progressives want to promote the whole development of the child – physically, cognitively, socially, and emotionally. Topics should arise from the child's interests, not the teachers' goals. (Edmunds et al., 2015, p. 223)

[Kilpatrick] argued that the best learning happens when children, in response to their own curiosity, seek answers to problems in their environment. (Edmunds et al., 2015, p. 224)

CHAPTER 17

# John: Transformational Teacher from Vietnam to Rural BC

John grew up in Salmon Arm, in the interior of British Columbia (BC). John's dad was an accountant and his mother a secretary. He is the youngest of three siblings. His two older sisters did not become teachers. One became a nurse and the other does bookkeeping. In fact, there are no teachers in John's family. He is the only one. John fondly recalls his grade 5 teacher who sparked his interest in outdoor education. John's grade 5 teacher was inspiring, but he struggled in high school and nearly dropped out. High school can be a very difficult and challenging time for many students. Moreover, a great deal of learning happens outside the classroom. Formal schooling is not for everyone. So, teaching was not John's initial career plan. Instead, John studied hospitality management at Thompson Rivers University (TRU). But this career did not suit John.

John loves the outdoors. He has lived and worked in various tourist spots across BC. Before coming a BC certified teacher John taught English as a Second Language (ESL) to children and adults for a number of years in Vietnam, including two extended stays. But it was only during his second work experience in Vietnam, that he decided to go back to school to become an elementary teacher. When John returned to Canada, he applied to TRU's Bachelor of Education Program (BEd Elementary). After two years of study, John graduated in the spring of 2018 and began teaching immediately. John entered the teaching profession in his thirties. While many teacher candidates are in their early twenties, there are many individuals who enter teaching later in life. In fact, the average age of TRU teacher candidates is over thirty. The mature students bring with them rich life experiences. They are exemplary, dedicated, a pleasure to teach, and are often are the most memorable. Such is the case here. As a result of his coursework at TRU, John is committed to teaching for social justice and environmental education. John has travelled extensively and has experienced many different places from crowded cities in Vietnam to BC's small rural communities. These experiences have had a major impact on his emerging educational philosophy.

### 1     Teaching in Vietnam

In 2011, at the age of 27, John went to Vietnam with his girlfriend who was on a TRU study abroad program. At that time, John was unsure what he wanted to do for a living and was unprepared for his teaching. He did not get much guidance, nor did he have the necessary *teacher toolkit* or educational foundations to build upon. John did not enjoy teaching ESL. It seemed that most of the ESL schools were more interested in making money rather than promoting effective learning. Nevertheless, John spent more than three months in Vietnam during his first stay. Returning to Vietnam the following year, he chose to stay for nearly another four years, as he had a very different, positive teaching experience. This motivated John to pursue teaching as a career. What was different the second time? First of all, John had the opportunity to teach in a large Hanoi primary school that helped him develop his teaching skills and this experience facilitated effective pedagogies of practice. By teaching the same lesson to more than 20 different classes, he didn't have to focus on lesson planning but rather could focus on improving his teaching strategies and nurturing students' learning. John really enjoyed teaching his hundreds of grade 1 students at this large primary school in Vietnam. Imagine a huge school with dozens of classes in each grade level and thousands of students all in one institution?! But in teaching the same lesson over and over to more than twenty different grade 1 classes, John had the opportunity to hone his teaching skills. John had plenty of practice.

Then, after five months of teaching in Hanoi, John moved away from the crowded, polluted city of Hanoi, to Da Nang on the east central coast of Vietnam, where he experienced a number of different schools before choosing one that was truly exceptional. It was at this ESL school John met Mr. Hai, who was an amazing mentor. Mr. Hai shared with him a student-centred approach to learning. John learned that teaching was a lot more satisfying when students were actively engaged in their learning. John also learned a great deal more about effective teaching strategies from this knowledgeable teacher. John's mentor gave him a great deal of guidance and improved his self-confidence. "I owe everything to him... I realized then how little I really knew about teaching," said John. This transcultural experience facilitated John's growth, both personally and professionally.

> You could tell Mr. Hai cared about the quality of education. During my interview demo lesson, I immediately noticed the impressive speaking abilities of the students in comparison to other centres I'd worked for. This provided me immediate evidence that Mr. Hai knew what he was doing, which made me receptive to his criticism and suggestions. The

school also provided many special opportunities to help students in need. It was chosen and funded by the U.S. State Department to provide English lessons to underprivileged students in Danang. It also provided sponsored students from the countryside with opportunities to come to the city for intensive summer immersion programs. Teaching those programs and seeing the effort, progress, and gratefulness from those students helped spark a real passion for teaching.

Mr. Hai would observe my lessons and scrutinize everything I did. He rubbed lots of teachers the wrong way and caused many teachers to leave because he was so critical. While it was sometimes hard to face the criticism he gave after putting so much effort into coming up with innovative lesson plans, it was constructive, and I was determined to improve. After a few months, once I caught on to the student-centred language pedagogy he was pushing for and came up with numerous ideas to implement it, it was smooth sailing. After a while, he approached me to become a supervisor. I declined, but I agreed to working extra hours as a teacher-trainer while still teaching classes of my own. I taught many of the same students for about three years, seeing them progress from absolute beginners to fully conversational speakers. To me, there is no greater motivator than to see the progress of students.

## 2 Teaching in Rural BC

During John's first three years of teaching experience in BC schools, he has endured many challenges, including teaching in a rural setting with difficult students and the COVID-19 pandemic. Upon graduation, John was immediately hired by Kamloops School District 73. As is common these days, John gained a foothold into the school district as a teacher teaching on call (TTOC). TRU grads are sought after and often get TTOC positions upon graduation. Being a TTOC enables novice teachers to experience many different schools, grades, classes and teaching environments. In his first year, John taught all sorts of classes from kindergarten through grade 12. This was great experience. Filling in for two teachers, first teaching a grade 4 and then a grade 3/4 split was very rewarding. He had an extended time with the same groups of students while covering these teachers. A highlight was that John ended up planning a multi-day field trip for students. Part of this involved fundraising through a "cardboard carnival." Inspired by the YouTube video "Caine's Arcade," students created functioning carnival games out of cardboard and ran a carnival for the whole school, complete with a prize booth and hot dog stand. The carnival brought in over $1000. Both the carnival and the camp were a success. It gave John a great sense of accomplishment. It is one of his best memories from his first year of teaching in BC.

John's second year of teaching was not as successful. The school is in a rural setting. It is a village. He taught a rambunctious group of grade 6 students. It made John question whether he wanted to continue as a teacher. It was very tough. There were many students with challenging behavioural issues. On the first day of school, in the wake of Prime Minister Trudeau's "Black Face Scandal" one boy decided to paint his hands with a black felt marker and to parade around the classroom using the N-word. John told him to stop. But he continued. So, John brought this student to the office. The boy placed his ink-stained hands on the walls, and all over the school, on the way to the office. This was a horrible start to a difficult year. In a sense, the COVID-19 pandemic was a welcome release for John, who was struggling to manage this difficult class. Not much learning took place during the final months of the school year, as students were not in the right frame of mind to learn in a regular classroom, let alone online. Throughout the year, defiance and disruption were ongoing daily issues with numerous students and it greatly affected the other students' ability to learn and John's ability to adequately teach. There were issues like fist fights and vaping.

One particularly memorable and scary incident occurred soon after John had dismissed his class at the end of the day. A few minutes later, a student came into the classroom with blood absolutely everywhere, leaving a trail all down the hallway, and drenching his face and clothes. He had accidentally been hit with a bat and tore his nose open. His mom came to the school and together they took an ambulance to the city hospital. John followed them there to give them a ride back afterwards. In the end, the student was fine after some stitches, but that was a terrifying moment – at first John had no idea what had happened! It's also an example of how unpredictable the job of teaching can be.

John's third year was better. His grade 5/6 split class of 23 students did not have as many behavioural issues and his students seem more inclined to learn, however there were more diverse educational and socio-emotional challenges, including supporting non-readers, COVID-19 related student anxiety, students who refused to participate in any activity, students prone to extreme emotional outbursts, and a student going through gender identity challenges. The 2020–2021 year was more like a regular school year, compared to the previous year when COVID-19 significantly interrupted student learning. With the pandemic, students must stay in their cohorts. John wears a mask, but the students do not. Students do group work. The school has staggered recess time, so that students stay with their cohort at all times.

John's lessons have dealt with various meaningful topics including units on media literacy, underground to Canada, slavery, civil rights and residential schools. He has even tackled controversial and contemporary issues with his students such as the Black Lives Matter movement. John notes while he enjoys teaching these lessons, he thinks that the social studies curriculum in grades 5 and 6 might be better suited for a higher grade.

## 3    Educational Philosophy

Below is John's educational philosophy statement articulated as a teacher candidate in 2017. It is interesting to compare it with his reflections four years later.

### 3.1    *Student-Centred Active Learning*

I am a firm believer that children learn best by "doing." The days of encyclopedic learning and rote memorization are over. Children are not blank slates that we can simply fill will knowledge (Sewell, 2002). They all learn differently and construct their own knowledge. I believe our job, as educators, is to facilitate their construction of knowledge through a differentiated and active learning environment, to scaffold their learning and to provide them with the tools they need to make sense of the world around them. I believe it is important for them to do so through inquiry and critical thinking, and the best way to facilitate this is by providing hands-on opportunities for students to learn about the things that interest them. I hope to incorporate ideas such as project-based learning (PBL) and Genius Hour into my teaching to stimulate student interest in the learning process and provide real-world application that will help students beyond the classroom. If a student is excited about learning, it can be difficult to pull them away from their work, which I feel is the beginning of a road to success. I also believe that an active learning environment can form the backbone of a universal design for learning (UDL), by providing multiple means of representation, expression, and engagement.

### 3.2    *Cooperative Learning*

I am a strong proponent of cooperative learning. I have a tendency to incorporate more cooperative learning activities into my teaching than the average teacher. I have found in my own teaching experience; the majority of students prefer cooperative learning over teacher-centred or individual learning. A comparative study of fourth-grade classrooms by Stelt (1995) also found that 84% of students preferred cooperative learning over teacher-centred learning.

I feel that cooperative learning has the potential for greater academic success as a result of the following additional benefits:

It develops critical thinking skills by having students consider and incorporate other students' perspectives into their learning. It builds their social skills and cooperation skills. It can provide opportunities to teach empathy and to develop positive and critical peer feedback skills. It can give students an opportunity to practice leadership skills. It is conductive to differentiated learning when group members can take on different tasks. It encourages peer support, lessening the reliance on the teacher for support.

While I like to incorporate cooperative learning into my lessons, I also recognize that some students prefer to work alone, and all students need opportunities to demonstrate their ability to work alone. Therefore, I do try to balance cooperative learning with individual learning.

### 3.3   *Critical Thinking and Metacognition*

Critical thinking has been a buzzword in our education system for several decades, to the point where its actual meaning has become distorted (Howe, 2000). I think it has become more of general term that is simply interpreted as thinking deeply about an idea and considering alternate perspective, yet critical thinking is so much more than that. It involves scientific reasoning, cognitive strategizing, conscientious judgements, relevance, and intellectual engagement (Howe, 2000). I intend to foster critical thinking through debates, cooperative learning, self-reflection, group discussion, inquiry, practical application of knowledge, cross-curricular application of knowledge, and the facilitation of metacognition. I think metacognition is such a key skill to have, yet is not given enough attention, with many teachers lacking sufficient knowledge about metacognition (Veenman, Van Hout-Wolters, & Afflerbach, 2005). I believe when students can understand how they learn, and reflect on their learning, they can discover what learning techniques are most beneficial to them and take more control of their own learning.

### 3.4   *Cross-Curricular and Technological Integration*

I feel that cross-curricular integration and technological integration are significant factors to consider when creating lessons and unit plans. In the past, subjects were always taught in isolation, but there has been a shift away from this approach for a valid reason. Application of knowledge outside school usually requires the crossing and blending of knowledge from various subjects and disciplines. I believe that teaching subjects in isolation leads to superficial learning and students may not see the practical application of what they are learning. When students can make cross-curricular connections, they can see the value and application of what they are learning in relation to other subjects and concepts. I feel there is nothing that can't be integrated in some way with another subject, and I think cross-curricular integration is also a way to be efficient and maximize use of class time.

I also embrace the integration of technology into all subjects. Although I enjoy integrating technology and try to explore new ways to utilize it the classroom, I also approach technological integration with caution. I recognize the importance of setting guidelines, and not using technology simply because it is there. With each use of technology in the classroom, I carefully consider how it will contribute to the objectives of the lesson. "An individual has not started living until he can rise above the narrow confines of his individualistic concerns to the broader concerns of all humanity" (Martin Luther King, Jr.).

## 3.5   *Multicultural Education*

The one subject matter that I am most passionate about teaching is multicultural education. In our education system, knowledge is controlled by a hidden curriculum that reinforces Eurocentric values, cultural hegemony, and an acceptance of racism and discrimination (Egbo, 2009). I am committed to changing this by going beyond a superficial glimpse of multiculturalism. As Shehla Burney (2012) puts it, multiculturalism often just "boils culture to curry and perogies" (p. 202). My ultimate goal will be to have the students realize and embrace what Ghosh and Abdi (2013) refer to as "a transculture of commonality across differences" (p. 167). I strive to reach this goal by facilitating student-centred discussion to empower and engage students, go beyond standard texts to the vast array of technological resources that can provide subaltern perspectives, and allow for intercultural collaboration. In the face of large-scale global conflicts stemming from misunderstanding and intolerance of the Other, I feel it is more crucial than ever to promote cultural understanding and global cooperation. I also intend to apply a similar approach to promote understanding in other aspects of diversity, including diverse ability, gender diversity, and sexual diversity.

When John was asked what if anything after three years of teaching has changed his educational philosophy. He indicated that while he still believes in those things, the realities of teaching have caused him to focus more on classroom management. Also, John has come to realize that students can't learn if they are coping with all sorts of issues beyond the classroom. Moreover, students need self-discipline. So, John has reluctantly had to revert to traditional methods to deal with various classroom management issues. Here are John's reflections after three years of teaching:

### 3.6    Student-Centred Active Learning

Ideally, yes, I still believe this is the right approach when possible, but it is hindered by the students' lack of independence and executive functioning skills. In a class with fewer challenges, I would fully maximize the amount of this type of learning, but with a class that struggles with behaviour, self-motivation, and dependence, I feel more time needs to be dedicated to direct instruction and building the foundational skills and executive functioning skills needed for student-centred projects and active learning. The longer I teach, the more I feel I am drifting from a progressive approach to a more traditional teaching approach.

### 3.7    Cooperative Learning

I have a much more balanced view now, in regard to cooperative versus individual learning. Again, this boils mostly down to behaviour. While the concept of cooperative learning is fantastic, I find students are often far less productive, as they are easily distracted, drift off-topic, and can often get too silly. Many opportunities for cooperative learning have come to a quick end when students are not able to show the responsibility to work with partners or groups. Many of the students prefer to work alone as well and will be stubborn and non-participative if put in a group.

### 3.8    Critical Thinking

While I still believe this is of extreme importance, especially in the current age of misinformation we live in, it has been more of a challenge than I ever expected to promote critical thinking. It's like pulling teeth trying to get students to answer any questions that involve their own thoughts and judgements, or providing logical reasoning, supporting details and evidence. Any open-ended questions usually end with me spoon feeding them a possible answer rather than them coming up with their own answers.

### 3.9    Technological Integration

My stance has changed a bit on this. I still think it's important for students to learn to use technology, and I recognize its potential to aid students and motivate them. However, after teaching a couple students with severe addiction to technology and knowing that so many students stay up until 2 am or 3 am every night playing on their devices, I'm more hesitant to integrate technology into everything we do in class.

Other aspects of my philosophy have stayed more or less the same.

CHAPTER 18

# Mrs. Henderson: Northern BC Inner-City School Experience

## 1    Background and Cultural Context

In early 2001, the newly established fiscally conservative Liberal government of British Columbia (BC) initiated sweeping neo-liberal educational reforms, including various measures to drastically change the education system. Teachers found themselves under attack. BC teacher salaries fell short of other provinces and salary increases were not keeping up with inflation. Class sizes went up. Provisions for special needs students and individual education plans were not respected. The gains that had been achieved through many rounds of contract negotiations over the years were systematically stripped from contracts between teachers and school districts across the province. Contracts between teachers and local school districts were under dispute. In a heavy-handed approach, the BC government exercised centralized control over the education system. In 2014, the labour dispute escalated and there was a province-wide strike. Two years later, the Supreme Court of Canada ruled that the BC government was wrong in striping away the class size provisions and other benefits from contracts, that teacher unions had fought hard to obtain. So, things changed dramatically as a result. Suddenly, there was a teacher shortage, and it was much more desirable to become a teacher. More classes were opened up as class sizes returned to their previous caps on enrolment. In the years that followed, more and more students chose to enter teaching as a profession in British Columbia.

In 2016–2019, it was a very good time to become a teacher. There were more applicants than ever before and enrolments at Thompson Rivers University (TRU) went up. While there was only one cohort of elementary students in 2014–2017, the program returned to two cohorts in 2018–2020 as was the case prior to 2014. There were many teaching opportunities throughout the province. Teaching in British Columbia schools has gone through some tough times in recent decades but most TRU teacher candidates readily find employment. Nevertheless, it is still competitive, and many recent graduates have to start their teaching careers as part-time teachers or teachers on call in order to get hired eventually as full time faculty with tenure. Of course, a lot changed in 2020, with the COVID-19 pandemic. Teachers suddenly had to pivot their lessons and make drastic changes but that is another story.

It is not unusual for teachers to have to move in order to find work. The situation for young novice teachers is often challenging. Many teacher education students graduate with large student loans and debt. Financial matters often are front and centre when it comes to deciding where to teach. School districts in remote locations have traditionally offered lucrative signing bonuses and incentives such as accelerated salary increments. However, schools up north have always had difficulties attracting and recruiting teachers.

So, perhaps it is not surprising that when Mrs. Henderson graduated from TRU in spring of 2019, after a brief stint as a teacher teaching on call (TTOC) in the Kamloops School District 73 and in nearby Merritt, she was offered a full-time teaching position in Northern BC, starting in October 2019. Her first year was tough but rewarding. The stories shared here illustrate the pervasive gap between pre-service and in-service teaching. In addition, the various challenges of teaching within an inner-city school are highlighted. Moreover, the pivot of teachers due to the COVID-19 pandemic is also touched upon.

Immediately, after graduation, in the spring of 2019, Mrs. Henderson worked as a TTOC for Merritt School District 58 and then briefly as a TTOC in Kamloops School District 73, before moving up north. Mrs. Henderson started working full-time in October 2019, after Thanksgiving, teaching a grade 4/5 split class to a very challenging group of students. In her second year of teaching, Mrs. Henderson noted that ten students had been placed on an Individualized Education Plan (IEP) and there were at least as many that should have been on an IEP. Some students had been diagnosed with Attention Deficit Hyperactivity Disorder (ADHD) and others exhibited significant behaviour problems. This inner-city school in northern BC caters to blue-collar, working class citizens – many parents do not value education and want nothing to do with schooling. There is not much diversity, but more than half the students are Indigenous. Socio-economic-status and poverty of students is clearly a factor. Needless to say, COVID-19 also had major impact.

As some of the stories that follow are troubling, contentious, highly confidential, and potentially threatening, the names of students have been changed to protect their identities. Mrs. Henderson (also a pseudonym) shared several critical incidents in her first year of teaching involving challenging parents, students, and staff.

## 2 Stories of Resistance and Resilience

Mrs. Henderson grew up in Kamloops. She is the middle child of three siblings and daughter of a middle-class Indo-Canadian family. She credits her supportive parents and teachers for her academic success. When Mrs. Henderson's husband got a promotion, she followed him up north. They both were keen to experience life outside their hometown of Kamloops. Their newly adopted city in northern BC, seemed like a good fit. Nevertheless, on Mrs. Henderson's second day of teaching on call, she was posted to a school that everybody had warned her about. She was told to stay away from that area. It was a huge and imposing elementary school with two floors. But immediately, Mrs. Henderson was impressed by the welcoming atmosphere of the office staff and the vibrant, energetic vice-principal. Moreover, the faculty proved to be strong teachers who were passionate about teaching and helping students in need. It was not just about the curriculum or teaching subjects. Teachers really cared about students. There was a great sense of community. It was something she had not seen in her previous experiences.

Mrs. Henderson was asked to teach physical education (PE), which was not her subject speciality but nevertheless, she felt confident as she had always been active in sports. On her very first day at this inner-city school, she taught two gym classes and then later that day, she was offered a contract to teach PE, prep and ELL as well as a grade 4/5 split class on Fridays. Mrs. Henderson was hired as a gym prep and English Language Learning (ELL) teacher – so she would take classes to the gym during classroom teachers' preparation time. For her ELL duties, she assisted Indigenous students or those who did not have English as their first language to work on their reading and writing skills.

Two different situations can happen if a student is sent home for an undetermined amount of time – either a parent meeting needs to happen (and often that difficult) or the student needs to see a doctor before returning if the issues are beyond what teachers and parents are able to assist with. According to Mrs. Henderson, this situation has resulted in some positive changes for some students' parents who needed to take their child to a doctor to get medication that would have continued to be overlooked had the school not taken that approach.

3   Challenging Students

In the early days of teaching, Mrs. Henderson was faced with a belligerent student, Calvin who refused to sit down. Mrs. Henderson had not been informed of Calvin's background and severe behavioural issues. In retrospect, it would have been helpful if Mrs. Henderson had received some sort of briefing about all her students. Calvin's actions were impacting the learning of other students. So, Mrs. Henderson attempted to deal with the situation. After about 20 minutes of trying to get Calvin to sit down, she made an effort to contact the youth worker for assistance, by calling the office. But Calvin followed Mrs. Henderson and grabbed her arm as she was about to make the call, saying "Don't you dare call the office!" In that moment, Mrs. Henderson felt a little fearful, but she told Calvin, in a firm voice, "You need to let go. This could get a lot worse for you." Nothing had prepared Mrs. Henderson for this sort of threat or for the non-compliance of students. This was new territory! Calvin continued to misbehave and refused to sit down. This carried on for another 25 minutes or so. Finally, the youth care worker arrived as none of the administrators were available at that time. Calvin was escorted by the youth care worker to the special "time out room" and eventually calmed down. Calvin spent most of the morning there under the watchful eye of the youth care worker but eventually returned to the classroom. Thankfully, there are lots of hands-on play activities available in this special room. The school has found various ways to effectively deal with classroom behavioural issues. Nevertheless, in reflecting on this critical incident, Mrs. Henderson feels she should have done a "room clear" to immediately give this student the chance to settle down away from his peers.

## 4  Challenging Parents: Dealing with Difficult Parents in a Small Community

On one of her first days of teaching, Mrs. Henderson had to cope with a serious and violent student misbehaviour. At this time, Bob was not medicated for his ADHD. In gym class, he was hitting other students. Mrs. Henderson told him to stop numerous times, but he continued to lash out at others. Mrs. Henderson escorted Bob to the office. A few days later, when Mrs. Henderson inquired about disciplinary action, the vice-principal said "Don't worry about it. The principal is dealing with it." But in the meantime, Bob's mother had complained, indicating that she felt her son was being picked on and discriminated against, stemming from the fact he had ADHD. This parent was upset and placed all the blame on Mrs. Henderson for this incident. As a first-year teacher, Mrs. Henderson felt particularly vulnerable. She felt this parent and other parents would likely see her as not prepared and inexperienced. As a novice teacher, Mrs. Henderson did not have much experience with these sorts of students, so she questioned whether she had done the right thing. Of course, if a student is hitting other students, some sort of action must be taken. This can't be tolerated! So, the administrators backed her up, completely. She had done the right thing after all.

Another challenging situation with difficult parents, arose in her second year of teaching, when Mrs. Henderson had to deal with the fallout from a critical incident involving staff and students at her school. In a close community, it is not uncommon for teachers and parents to come into contact with one another in various contexts, but this was an exceptional case. One of Mrs. Henderson's students had a parent who worked as an Education Assistant (EA) in the school. The EA in dealing with Kelly, a defiant student, chose to physically direct the student. Kelly was sent home. Kelly's parents were very upset with Mrs. Henderson and the EA in how this situation was dealt with. They tried to get Mrs. Henderson fired for allegedly picking on Kelly and complained to the school district. Unfortunately, the unpleasantries also carried over to Mrs. Henderson's husband's workplace because Kelly's father is a co-worker. This speaks to the reality that in a smaller community, "everyone seems to know everyone else" and there are connections that go outside the school. But in this case, the actions of Kelly's parents clearly crossed a line and caused a chain reaction of serious outcomes with implications for everyone involved. As a result, the EA was transferred to another school and the students involved are not in Mrs. Henderson's class anymore.

## 5  Challenging Times: COVID-19 Trauma and Stress

In Mrs. Henderson's second year of teaching, the school was better prepared to deal with the challenges presented by the COVID-19 pandemic. Nevertheless, a significant challenge is that elementary school teachers only work with the same students in their cohort bubble. With many students on IEPs, Mrs. Henderson lamented she had lost the two EAs that were assigned to her special needs students. One autistic student, who is high on the spectrum, has to make do without an EA. Another student was sent home for 2 weeks, because he was constantly trying to physically hurt himself. One student was physically violent towards another staff member and was dealing with the trauma of losing his father who was murdered. There are a lot of mean grade 6 and 7 students who pick on the grade 4 and 5 students. But it is difficult to break free of this situation as they are part of the same learning group. Students are constantly having emotional breakdowns after recess because of what is being said on the playground.

A new issue has evolved as a result of a zero-tolerance policy to student misbehaviour. If a student misbehaves, they are sent home. They are not allowed to return to school until a parent comes to school to discuss the situation and to form an action plan with the administration. However, that poses a serious challenge, as many parents do not respect teachers and are sometimes as non-compliant as their children. This has resulted in one student being sent home and not attending school at all. While this student may end up in some form of alternate schooling, she will likely fall through the cracks. Other students might follow this same fate unless this school policy changes. Mrs. Henderson worries about them.

## 6   Teaching Philosophy Final Reflections

Reflection is really important. The one lesson from teacher education that has stuck with Mrs. Henderson is how important reflection is to teaching. Mrs. Henderson's teaching philosophy changed during her first year of teaching. Mrs. Henderson's philosophy has changed more to an inclusion/equity approach. She has had a few students living with Autism and high on the spectrum, so it became her mission to ensure they were actively engaged in classroom learning at all times.

While a teacher candidate, as part of her coursework and exit portfolio, she created an educational philosophy statement. Here is what she wrote:

> Plato is arguably the most well-known philosopher of all-time. He created the Athens Academy, which was the first institute for higher learning, essentially setting the foundation for educational learning to spread throughout the world into what we see today. While Plato's teachings need to badly be tweaked to incorporate people of all genders, the meaning behind Plato's words is what I draw inspiration from. As a future educator, I firmly believe that I will be responsible for shaping both children and youth into responsible, intellectual and caring beings. Plato believed that, "knowledge will not come from teaching but from questioning." He did not believe in students learning trivial facts, but instead learning about the world and looking at a question as a quest to find meaning and understanding. Personally, I've been in many class settings where I've been required to study and memorize tidbits of information in order to get a great grade and then after the termination of the course no longer require much, if any, of the information in question. Thankfully, I've been lucky to be in classrooms where I've had teachers take a different approach, where they challenged us to not only find the answers but apply it to real-world settings and allow us to find use for this information or learning-processes throughout life. My teaching philosophy would be to create this type of environment for my students, an inquiry-based learning environment. By creating a safe judgement free environment for my students, I strongly believe inquiry-based learning would benefit all types of learners that I will encounter. Giving the students choices when

it comes to learning will create a sense of empowerment and allows the student to take ownership of their learning. Additionally, progressive education is a view of education that emphasizes the need to learn by doing and being hands-on. It represents schools being an opportunity for children to develop as individuals. John Dewey, an educational philosopher, believed that human beings learn through a 'hands-on' approach. In the case study, "Just in Time," in our textbook, Case Studies in Educational Foundations, we read about how quickly technology is taking over in schooling systems and just how beneficial it can be for students. I am a strong believer in technology and the comfort and ease of access to information it can bring to students when used responsibly. During my times in different classrooms, I have seen students be happy and confident when they are able to use a Chromebook or iPad to aid in their learning. I want to create a classroom environment that embraces the ever-changing world of technology and have my students feel comfortable doing the same.

CHAPTER 19

# Sean: Primary Teacher amidst the COVID-19 Pandemic

Sean was born in Winnipeg and spent the first 12 years of his life there. His family moved to Kamloops in 2005. Sean attended junior high school and high school in Kamloops, BC. He then went to Simon Fraser University before transferring to Thompson Rivers University (TRU). Sean volunteered to coach football at his old high school and also worked in summer sports camps at TRU. At this time, Sean connected again with his teachers and coaches, who motivated him to go into teaching. Sean enjoyed coaching football. He decided teaching was a good career choice as Sean had always had great teachers and it seemed like a good fit for his interest in sports. Sean wanted to share some of that passion with his students. Sean entered the TRU Elementary Teacher Education Program in 2016 and graduated with his Bachelor of Education degree in spring 2018. He started teaching for the Kamloops School District (SD73) in September 2018.

Sean has had a number of short-term teaching positions, teaching a variety of students from kindergarten to grade 5. He recently was offered a full-time position teaching a split class of grade 3 and 4. Interestingly, most of his teaching has been to younger students in the early primary grades. While he expected to teach older students and his practicum experiences were in the upper intermediate and middle school years, Sean enjoys teaching grade 3 and 4, which is what he is teaching now in his third year of teaching.

Sean enjoys seeing the world through the eyes of young children. He mentioned that children provide us with a unique perspective. It helps us to remember what it was like to be that age and to better understand the world we live in. Sean's educational philosophy has not changed much over the past few years. The core values remain the same. However, Sean indicated that classroom management is critically important. Before a teacher can effectively teach a class, it is important to have the necessary classroom management skills in place first.

## 1   Educational Philosophy

### 1.1   *Importance of a Philosophy*
For me, the importance of a teaching philosophy for a teacher is just like a coach having a coaching philosophy. It outlines the things you believe in, grounds

you when things get difficult, and sets "goals and guide practice" (Stribling et al., 2015). I believe that informing your students about your teaching philosophy is important in setting expectations for the classroom.

### 1.2  *Progressivism*

One component to my teaching philosophy is progressivism. Progressivist philosophy is a "child-centred philosophy emphasizing problem solving while capitalizing on students curiosity and creative self-expression" (Edmunds, 2015). This theory paints teachers not as talking heads at the front of a classroom, but as facilitators of education whose goal is to promote learning in children. Progressivism incorporates open-ended learning for students which grants them the ability to study certain things that interest them. This not only leads to deeper thinking and engagement from students but makes them an active part in their own learning.

### 1.3  *Critical Thinking/Media Literacy*

Going forward in the 21st century, I believe that teachers need to teach students to be critical thinkers. It is their duty to help the next generation of citizens to critically analyze and explore all the information that students are bombarded with daily on social media, TV, and the Internet. Teachers need to instruct students to:

> Tell me and I forget. Teach me and I remember. Involve me and I learn. (Benjamin Franklin)

> Kids don't remember what you teach them. They remember what you are. (Jim Henson)

Students should be detectives when thinking critically about media. This follows the method proposed by John Dewey. He believes that people must scientifically examine any truths for further interrogation (Edmunds, 2015). The one thing teachers must avoid when teaching media literacy and critical thinking, is not to infer too much of their own opinions on their students and allow them to interpret things themselves.

### 1.4  *Inquiry-Based Learning*

Inquiry-based learning (IBL) is a deviation of progressivism. According to Avsec (2015), "inquiry-based learning (IBL) is an inductive leaning strategy that enables learners to construct and process knowledge, develop reasoning skills, and to increase interest and learning motivation." IBL combines aspects from both progressivism and critical thinking by enabling multi-faceted learning, as well as critical thinking. An important aspect to IBL is the inclusion of manipulative's, and the ability to explore phenomena. Primary teachers that use IBL must be sure to guide their students through the IBL process, and scaffold it to other areas of learning. I believe that inclusion in the classroom should be a part of every teacher's philosophy. Canada is a proud multicultural, diverse nation; and our classrooms should reflect our society as best it can. When possible, our classrooms should include people of different races, ethnicities, and physical and cognitive capabilities. Not only is it important to include these individuals, but it is of equal importance to inform the "normal" students about other people's differences and the importance of including them in society. The British Columbia School Act specifically states that it is the teacher's responsibility to "enable all learners to develop their individual potential and to acquire the knowledge, skills, and attitudes needed to contribute to a healthy, democratic, and pluralistic society" (Gnidec, 2008).

Overall, Sean indicated that not much has changed in his educational philosophy, written as a student, a few years ago, but he wished to add some noteworthy points after several years in the profession:

> Firstly, I have realized that much of what children are exposed to by the media (both news and social media), come directly from the parents up to a certain age, and that often the parent's opinions or biases toward news, or social media, is directly reflected in the opinions of how younger students feel about a topic. I know that as a kid, I often had similar views as my parents. This can often lead to a spreading of misinformation in the classroom, playground, or within social circles. I have had to have discussions with my class, and individually, quite a few times this year after heated debates about the existence of religious figures, or false political information broke out. As a professional, I must be careful not to sway the students either way of an argument and potentially catch heat from parents if they disagree with my point of view, but I also don't want the students to be misinformed on an important topic.
>
> Secondly, one thing that I have found out more this year than ever before, which falls under my "Inclusion" portion, is that it is important to teach students the difference between equity and equality. As stated below, my class is full of diverse learners and as a result, has forced me to adapt the work assigned. As children are usually very observant, they notice when a peer of the same grade group, without a visual physical or learning disability, is given less to do on the same/similar assignment. At the beginning of the year, I spoke to my students about equity versus

equality, and its importance in a learning environment. I used a metaphor about people riding bikes and that we wouldn't give children or someone in a wheelchair the same size, or type of bike, that a person such as myself would ride since they couldn't reach the pedals, handlebars, or operate it properly; however, if we give them bikes that fit their physical requirements, everyone can ride bikes together. I then told them the same goes with schoolwork. The students bought in, and understood the metaphor, and we've never had issues with that since. Most have become kinder and more understanding children as a result!

## 2    Kindergarten Teacher

Sean made good connections, in particular at one local elementary school, as a teacher on call, which led to his first long-term teaching position. For several months, from January 2020 through spring break in March 2020, Sean taught kindergarten in SD 73. The first thing he noticed was that the children seemed to not have much structure and organization. For example, there were issues in terms of where they were to sit during story time. The children said things like "You're in my bubble. Move!" So, Sean used tape to mark out a grid on the floor, with names, to give students a sort of seating plan. In addition, he initiated some routines, more structure, and organization to help manage students' behaviours. He let students have some choices in terms of what groups they would be working with by having them choose a card, much like playing a card game. These routines were well received by the children who reacted well to Sean's leadership. Sean quickly gained their respect. Sean was able to focus on literacy and numeracy. He made learning fun but also meaningful. Unstructured play in kindergarten is fine but children also need to be given scaffolding to be successful in school.

Given the fact Sean is a young male in his twenties with no children of his own, it might seem a stretch to be well suited as a kindergarten teacher. But when asked if there were any problems with skeptical parents, and whether parents questioned his ability and experience with headstrong five and six-year-olds, Sean indicated that there were no issues at all, and parents were receptive. Moreover, he mentioned that the children seemed to respect his authority. As Sean is tall with a commanding presence – maybe that had something to do with it! Sean made it clear to his students that he was in charge. Sean used a "three strikes and you're out" system which came into play when one girl threw a tantrum. The parents were supportive. It seemed to work.

## 3  Challenges of the Pandemic – Working at the Essential Services School

During the COVID-19 pandemic, in spring 2020, schools were shut down for several months. Teachers had to pivot to online learning and alternate modes of delivery. However, essential service workers like doctors, nurses, emergency responders, grocery store clerks, and others, continued to work. So, their children needed a safe place to learn as home-schooling was not an option for many people. Sean and two other teachers were hired in temporary contracts to provide schooling for children of essential workers. Sean was responsible for a multi-grade class comprised of a kindergarten student, two grade 1s, a grade 3 and a grade 5 student. These students were very different from one another. It was challenging to find lessons and activities that could be effective for each of them. In particular, during the first few weeks, it was really tough as teachers were not given much guidance… There were 12 desks in the classroom, separated from each other by 2 metres. As soon as children arrived, Sean let them in and directed the students to wash their hands. There was a decision to break up siblings. There was pushback from parents. But no rationale was provided for why siblings would be kept apart. Teachers had to "hit the ground running" on the first day. Sean had to explain how to log onto the Chromebooks, safely physically distanced, when the younger students were still learning how to spell! In the mornings from 8:30 until noon, Sean acted as a learning facilitator. In the afternoons, it was time for other activities like outdoor play. This continued from April through June 2020. When the weather permitted and in May, when children were able to go outside, things improved.

## 4  Grade 3/4 Split Class

Sean was offered his first 1.0 full time equivalent (FTE) position teaching a split class of grade 3 and 4 at the same elementary school where he had taught kindergarten the year before. This school serves a wide range of students, over a large catchment area. Some students are bused from a great distance while others are within walking distance. Generally, the parents are middle-class, blue-collar workers. This elementary school is quite typical of schools in Kamloops, a city of 90,000 people. The staff of this school are young and energetic. Teachers are highly collegial. Administrators are strong leaders and supportive. Sean mentioned that he is comfortable seeking advice from all the teachers. Clearly, this school is well liked by staff and students. It has a good reputation in SD73. There are even two students who moved across town, and yet these young children take public transit to attend this school. It takes more than an hour by bus!

Of Sean's 20 students, exactly half are in each grade, but they are all at very different educational levels. There are 12 girls and 8 boys. Moreover, there are several special needs students, each with Individual Education Plans (IEPs) and some students that perhaps should be on IEPs but are not yet. This makes teaching very challenging. Nevertheless, split classes are quite common in SD 73 these days.

Sean recalled an interesting anecdote from his class that speaks to the notion that these students bring a unique perspective to learning. During read aloud at snack time, Sean was reading from "Double Fudge," a story about Christmas... There was a part that spoke to whether Santa Claus was real or not. Many of Sean's students still believe in Santa, so he did not want to do anything to "burst their bubble" or provoke a debate amongst students. He quickly skipped ahead to avoid a controversial topic! This is a good example of how teachers often have to make many decisions quickly and change their lessons on the spot. With-it-ness is an important skill for teachers.

Sean's learning cohort partner is very helpful. She is like a mentor to Sean. This teacher has more than 20 years of experience. Sean is teaching from a portable. This is another challenge. For example, there is no sink and there is a necessity for "long bathroom breaks" but at least it is not as cold as what Sean experienced as a child in Winnipeg. Due to the COVID-19 pandemic, students must use hand sanitizer regularly and stick to their cohort. While masks are not mandatory, students are encouraged to wear a mask. Hand washing and physical distancing is difficult to micro-manage but teachers are working hard to get students to comply with public health orders. While these are difficult times, Sean is enjoying the challenges he is facing and seems to be very well suited to teaching these children. Sean likes teaching the basics to students who are in the "sweet spot" age of grade 3 and 4. Teaching children literacy and numeracy is something that gives Sean much satisfaction. He is very happy in his new career as a primary school teacher. Sean feels he entered teaching at a good time. British Columbia's new curriculum focused on core competencies is a welcome change. Also, the integration of technology makes teaching easier. Sean mentioned that most of his classmates have also managed to find work as teachers in Kamloops and surrounding school districts. While BC teachers are not the highest paid teachers in Canada and the salaries fall short of neighbouring Alberta, Sean is content to stay in Kamloops. However, there are implications to moving to another school district, in particular seniority. In these uncertain times, teachers are encouraged to hold on to a coveted full-time teaching position. There is excellent job security and room for growth. Teaching is a great profession. Sean has found his niche.

CHAPTER 20

# Glen Hansman: Intermediate Teacher, Former BCTF President & LGBTQ Advocate

Glen Hansman was born and raised in North Bay, a city in Northeastern Ontario of just over 50,000 people. North Bay is located on the traditional territory of the Nipissing First Nations Peoples. Glen also lived in Ottawa and Montreal, and has lived in Vancouver, BC since he started teaching in 2000. Glen was part of the French Immersion phenomena that swept the nation in the 1980s. His memories of elementary schooling were generally good but Glen's experiences in high school were not all that positive, even though he was always a strong student. From an early age, as a young teen, Glen knew he was gay, but he felt alone. He came out in high school. Growing up queer in an intolerant society poses serious challenges for our youth. So, like some individuals who become teachers, Glen did not have any significant mentors or outstanding teachers to motivate him to choose a teaching career. Both homophobia and racism were very much tolerated by staff at the high school; Glen remembers many instances of bigoted comments being made by students, and teachers or other staff either ignoring the comments or further fueling them. In Glen's case, it was a strong sense of social justice, his fight for inclusion, and the desire to make things better for the next generation, that propelled him into teaching.

During his first year at Nipissing University, some mental health challenges that Glen had been dealing with for some time deteriorated significantly, and Glen decided to take a break from schooling. This break lasted a couple years, until he moved to Ottawa and entered Carleton University in 1995. At Carleton, Glen majored in English literature and obtained his undergraduate degree. As a student, he became involved in social activism and joined university clubs – including the lesbian, gay, bisexual, and transgender student group, which was active in trying to address homophobia and transphobia on campus. At this time, Glen also volunteered and worked with children in Ottawa schools, and became interested in teaching as a potential career. Glen felt strongly that he wanted to help disadvantaged queer youth in similar situations within high school. He saw teaching as an opportunity to make positive change in communities. So, Glen went to McGill to get his Bachelor of Education (Secondary) and to become certified as a teacher. Glen's long practicum, in a Montreal secondary school, teaching moral education and English literature, was a success but there was one critical incident. Glen's teaching included a grade 11 unit on diversity and inclusion. He planned a major event near the end of his practicum. He had invited presenters from an organization supporting lesbian, gay, bisexual, transgender and queer (LGBTQ) youth to facilitate a conversation about their experiences in school. However, on the morning of the event, he found out it was cancelled by the principal. Apparently, the parent committee, which held some governance power, had met the night before and had decided the topic was too controversial. Glen vowed to never let that happen again, and to find out exactly what his rights were as soon as he was hired by a school district. Upon graduation from McGill, Glen worked briefly as a Teacher Teaching on Call (TTOC) in Montreal before relocating to Vancouver, British Columbia, where he lives now with his husband. He has 22 years of teaching experience.

## 1     Challenges of a Novice Teacher in a Changing Political Climate

In the summer of 2000, Glen moved to Vancouver and in September of that year he began teaching for the Vancouver School District. Glen was disappointed that he did not get a call on the first day of school. But his luck changed that afternoon. Almost all his work as a TTOC ended up being in elementary schools, instead of secondary – and by the end of that September, an assignment he had teaching a grade 2 class ended up becoming a long-term contract, after the teacher he was subbing for did not return to work. After gaining a reputation as a competent teacher and developing rapport with his colleagues, Glen filled in for a number of other teachers at that school before being offered a permanent contract. At first, Glen worked as a resource teacher at the same school. Even though Glen did not have specialist training in special education, his teaching for social justice background, his empathy for disadvantaged students and his personal experience helped. He quickly learned the ropes. Glen credits much of his transformational teaching to excellent professional development opportunities offered by the Vancouver School Board (VSB). Also, Glen was fortunate to have great colleagues who were very generous with sharing their expertise.

Glen found his niche teaching elementary school students. Furthermore, Glen really liked the ebb and flow of the elementary school day and began to prefer it to what he experienced on his practicum, teaching high school. Relationship building with students was much deeper than in high school. Glen stayed at that school for six years. During that time Glen was a sponsor teacher for about a half-dozen University of British Columbia (UBC) special education student teachers. This was also an excellent professional development opportunity as mentor teachers often learn a great deal from their teacher candidates.

But the first decade of the new millennium was not without significant challenges for all BC teachers. As Glen was a new teacher and new to Vancouver he experienced the typical challenges of novice teachers, but the biggest challenge was the impending changing political climate for teachers. With a change in government in 2001, Gordon Campbell's Liberals with Christy Clark as the Minister of Education, soon gained an infamous reputation for being anti-union and anti-public education. The new government was decidedly not on the side of public sector workers – particularly those in the health sector and in education. This precipitated many changes to the British Columbia College of Teachers (BCCT) formed in the late 1980s. Teachers had gained a great sense of autonomy and professionalism in the 1990s, but this was quickly eroded by heavy-handed draconian measures taken by the Liberals. The new government was determined to wrestle more control of the education system from teachers and set out to do just that. Subsequently, there were immediate major impacts to education including the imposition of legislation that stripped collective agreements of any reference to class size, staffing ratios for specialist teachers, and many other provisions related to teachers' working conditions – the immediate impact of was the elimination of more than 4,000 teaching jobs across the province. Like many other new teachers, who were low in seniority, Glen got laid off. But thankfully, Glen was soon re-hired. Nevertheless, there were fewer staff having to struggle with larger class sizes and more students with special needs without adequate support.

Glen participated in various union events that were in reaction to the government's legislation. In January 2002, Glen took part in a massive teacher protest held at the parliament buildings in Victoria, invited along to this union event by a more senior colleague. It would be many years until this matter was resolved, though. This was not a great time to be entering the teaching profession. There were many teachers out of work in September 2002. These events acted as a catalyst to motivate Glen to become involved in the union and to help lead a new VSB committee on developing an anti-homophobia policy and action plan for the entire school district. Glen stepped up to help. It was an important catalyst to help Glen get involved with his local union. In February 2002 the VSB carried a policy as a result. Next, training then started for all Vancouver principals, vice principals, and counsellors – with Glen directly involved in facilitating these sessions. He also started to get more involved in other activities of his local union, making connections between the work he was doing in LGBTQ activism and the broader interests of the labour movement – particularly trying to advance positive changes for teachers and for students through collective bargaining. In the 2005–2006 school year there was a 2-week strike in reaction to further legislation from the provincial government that interfered in the collective bargaining process. Glen accepted a part-time job at the school board as the district's first anti-homophobia consultant, choosing to share this role with another teacher. Glen had to balance this with several roles including teaching and a released role with the Vancouver Elementary School Teachers' Association (VESTA). He had also started his graduate degree in education at the University of British Columbia. Glen became the VESTA president for a few years. He then got involved in social justice work at the provincial level and worked together with many other teacher locals in BC to advance a number of issues through the provincial union. This eventually led to Glen becoming a member of the provincial executive of the British Columbia Teachers' Federation (BCTF) in 2009, a vice president from 2010 through 2016, and president for three years starting in 2016. This was just prior to the landmark Supreme Court decision in favour of the BCTF against the BC Liberals to reinstate class sizes and the provisions striped from collective agreements in 2002.

## 2    British Columbia Teachers' Federation President Highlights

As BCTF president from 2016–2019, Glen led the union of 43,000 teachers and had the opportunity to visit all 60 school districts throughout BC, seeing firsthand the teaching and learning conditions in as many communities as possible – including remote and northern communities. During his time as vice president and as president, Glen met many teachers and networked with each of the nine BC teacher education programs, meeting key stakeholders across the province and working with several Ministers of Education and their ministerial staff on a complete overhaul of the provincial K-12 curriculum, a number of initiatives related to Indigenous education and reconciliation, significant changes to the teachers' pension plan, and school safety initiatives. He emphasized efforts to work across unions and teacher organizations through provincial, national, and international coalitions like the BC Federation of Labour, Canadian Labour Congress, the Canadian Teachers' Federation, and Education International.

A noteworthy achievement, Glen helped lead the fledgling sexual orientation and gender identity (SOGI) movement at a provincial level, working with others to have gender identity and gender expression added to the BC Human Rights Code and related education regulations for the whole province, and helped to create a climate that supported SOGI 123, a set of education resources for teachers to make schools more inclusive and a lot more accepting of students of different gender identities and sexualities.[1] While in 2004 there were only two districts with policies specifically addressing school climate and inclusion of LGBTQ students and staff; by 2019 all 60 school districts throughout BC had SOGI 123 and/or some comparable program and policies in place. This was not without some push-back from social conservatives in parts of the province, but the initiative has largely been successful.

As BCTF president in November 2016, Glen was present at the Supreme Court of Canada in Ottawa when, after a 14-year legal battle, the provincial government's 2002 legislation pertaining to teachers' working conditions was finally overturned. This led to the opening of negotiations with the provincial government, which Glen led, resulting in the return of about 4,000 teaching positions across BC by the following September. When he was a new teacher in the early 2000s, he never would have imaged that it would take so long to resolve this dispute – let alone that he would be president of the union when teachers finally won. In conjunction with a similar win by workers in BC's health sector, the decision in BC teachers' favour is a milestone case for workers' rights across Canada and has implications nation-wide.

All teachers should take advantage of professional development and leadership opportunities to venture outside their classrooms. In Glen's time as BCTF president, he was able to visit many First Nations communities to better understand Indigenous ways of knowing and being. These experiences bode well for his return to teaching.

## 3   Back in the Classroom: A Look to the Future

Glen is happy to be back in the classroom now as teaching is his passion. It is gratifying to be back in school now. In particular, Glen is drawn to the intermediate grades 5, 6 and 7. At the age of 48, Glen has at least another decade or more left of teaching before heading into retirement. This is an exciting time to be a teacher. With the new BC Curriculum focused on core competencies and integrated cross-curricular learning, teachers have many opportunities to engage students in meaningful learning. Glen is keen to further hone his teaching skills and to make a difference in the lives of his students. Things have changed a great deal in the past two decades. Glen notes great stives in human rights and school policies pertaining to anti-homophobia, anti-transphobia, and inclusion – though, as he points out, clearly there is much more to do to address the day-to-day experience of youth in schools, particularly LGBTQ youth, black, Indigenous and people of colour (BIPOC) youth, and youth with disabilities. Glen remains optimistic, though, and is inspired by the organizing that continues to happen by youth and teacher activists around the province.

Nevertheless, Glen notes that connecting youth to mental health services will be a priority in the coming years as kids are having to shoulder a lot of additional things now. Many children have experienced and will continue to experience trauma, and schools are not always adequately equipped to provide the supports that are needed. Moreover, there is still a great deal of mistrust among key stakeholders in education. Even with the change of government in 2017, still challenges remain – particularly when it comes to funding, ensuring adequate services to students in all schools, and properly planning for a post-pandemic future. We still have lots of work to do.

**Note**

1  See https://www.sogieducation.org/

# Afterword

*Cheryl Craig*

Edward Howe did not miss a beat in this book. His work is filled with diversities ranging from subject matter like Home Economics, Music, PE and Social Studies to positions having to do with Orientation and Gender Identification, Indigenous Education, and Special Education, spanning seven decades. Additionally, there are journeys within Canada (i.e., Nova Scotia → Northwest Territories → British Columbia), to Canada (from Colombia) and from Canada (to Japan, to Vietnam). Both urban and rural landscapes are represented, along with different decades of time and different continents of the world (North America/South America/Europe/Asia). For instance, readers learn about the pathways of teachers who began their careers in the 1950s through the 1980s including Hazel, a strong Chinese-Canadian, and other pioneers like Clare and Norma as well as Terry, Beverly, Bill, and Anne. Readers also come to know about a Japanese administrator (Ueda-Sensei), new educators in Japan (Mari, Ken) and Three Sensei (Novice, Mid-Career, Veteran) as well as the life of new primary Canadian teachers (John, Mrs. Henderson, and Sean) during the COVID-19 pandemic and the advocacy of a former BCTF President (Glen) and Administrator (Vessy) for LGBTQ issues. Alicia's narrative illustrates the myriad of challenges facing teachers pertaining to special education, equity, diversity, and inclusion. Readers are also afforded a glimpse into Indigenous perspectives with the addition of Carolyn and Marie's narratives of education and experience. Finally, Marie's detailed teaching journal (Appendix B) provides a window into the life of a novice teacher in her first year. Amidst this rich plurality of people, places and situations, the overarching takeaway point is that careers and lives are marked by passages, albeit not the same. Throughout this volume, Edward (Ted) Howe keeps his eye fully cast on life and career changes. We not only come to know particularities about his research participants and their experiences; we also learn about Ted whose parents were his first teachers and whose opportunity to teach in Japan greatly influenced the arc of his career and the contours of his life. In short, we learn about Ted's "I" (his self) *and* his "eye" (his inquiry into others' careers and lives). We leave this reading knowing that lives and careers may differ in their unfolding, but all unavoidably involve acculturation in a myriad of forms as Edward Howe so keenly has shown us – and in a way we are unlikely to forget.

APPENDIX A

# Critical Response Questions

### Chapter 1: Hazel
1. Why do you think Hazel considers herself Chinese and not Canadian?
2. How have things changed for women teachers since the 1950s?
3. What challenges do racialized teachers still face?

### Chapter 2: Ueda-sensei
1. How is the cultural context of teaching different in Japan?
2. What challenges did Japanese teachers face in the 1960s~1980s?
3. What aspects of Ueda-sensei do you admire or not admire? Why?

### Chapter 3: Clare
1. Why did Clare become a university instructor rather than a secondary teacher?
2. What elements of Clare's story pertain to equity, diversity, and inclusion?
3. How does gender play an important role in Clare's stories of experience?

### Chapter 4: Norma
1. Why did Norma become a teacher?
2. How has teaching changed over the many years of Norma's career?
3. What aspects of Norma's story resonated with your own experience?

### Chapter 5: Terry
1. How can teachers cope with systemic poverty and other social issues?
2. How is teaching in urban settings different from rural settings?
3. What aspects of Terry's story resonated with your own experience?

### Chapter 6: Beverly
1. Why did Beverly become a teacher? How important were her teachers?
2. Do teachers enter teaching because of positive schooling experiences? Why or why not?
3. How is the cultural and historical context of Beverly's experience abroad relevant?

### Chapter 7: Bill
1. Why did Bill become a socials teacher rather than a PE teacher?
2. Is it important for novice teachers to have a mentor? Why or why not?
3. What aspects of Bill's story resonated with your own experience?

### Chapter 8: Anne
1. Why did Anne become an administrator?
2. How does religion permeate classrooms?
3. What aspects of Anne's story resonated with your own experience?

### Chapter 9: Gloria
1. How might you use transcultural experiences in your own teaching?
2. Have you had a teacher who inspired you? Share your story of experience.
3. What aspects of Gloria's story resonated with your own experience?

### Chapter 10: Ted
1. Share a noteworthy story from your own education and experience.
2. What personal practical knowledge do you hold as a teacher?
3. What does it mean to be a transcultural teacher?

### Chapter 11: Vessy
1. In terms of sexuality and gender identity, how have attitudes and social norms changed since the 1990s?
2. If you were a gay teacher, would you come out? Why or why not?
3. How can teachers support LGBTQ students?

### Chapter 12: Alicia
1. How could Alicia's practicum experience be improved?
2. Would you consider a career other than public school teaching? Why or why not?
3. What are the challenges associated with teaching children with autism or ADHD?

### Chapter 13: Three Sensei
1. How is the cultural context of teaching in Japan different from Canada or elsewhere?
2. Would you like to teach abroad? Why or why not? Where?
3. What aspects of these teacher stories resonated with your own experience?

### Chapter 14: Mari and Ken
1. Why did Mari and Ken want to be English teachers?
2. What challenges did Mari and Ken face as novice teachers in Japan?
3. If you were in Ken's situation, what would you do?

### Chapter 15: Carolyn
1. Why is it important for us to study history, residential schools and the Sixties Scoop?

2. What are the Calls to Action of the TRC for teachers?
3. How can teachers Indigenize pedagogy? Give examples of Indigenous ways of knowing.

## Chapter 16: Marie
1. Why did Marie become a teacher?
2. What are challenges associated with teaching Indigenous children?
3. What aspects of Marie's story resonated with your own experience?

## Chapter 17: John
1. How did John's transcultural experience impact his teaching?
2. What challenges do rural teachers face?
3. How would you deal with student misbehaviour as described in this chapter?

## Chapter 18: Mrs. Henderson
1. What challenges did Mrs. Henderson face as a novice teacher?
2. How is teaching in an inner-city school different from other schools?
3. How would you deal with difficult parents as described in this chapter?

## Chapter 19: Sean
1. What issues might arise for male kindergarten teachers?
2. What challenges did teachers face as a result of the COVID-19 pandemic?
3. What aspects of Sean's story resonated with your own experience?

## Chapter 20: Glen
1. What issues might arise for LGBTQ teachers?
2. What challenges did Glen face as a novice teacher?
3. Why are teacher unions and strong teacher leaders important?

APPENDIX B

# Marie's Journal

### May 9, 2018

Today was my first day as a Teacher on Call (TOC) in Kamloops, BC. I was lucky enough to get a three-day consecutive assignment with a grade 2/3 class (my practicum was mainly with primary grades). I was also lucky enough to have a great bunch of students who made my day go by easily. There was the pushing of boundaries (sitting on or where they aren't supposed to at carpet; talking out of turn; taking advantage of bathroom breaks), but I was expecting exactly these behaviours. I dealt with all of these as they came and reminded them about their expectations in the classroom.

The day went by so quickly! I, of course, did not get through all of what was left behind for me by the regular classroom teacher (thank goodness she left behind detailed plans and prepped everything for me already!), but I followed my prepped plans as closely as I could. Tomorrow I hope to get through some more of the Language Arts that I did not get to today.

After school, the students were sent off with a "I'll see you all tomorrow," I marked what I went over for the day, and set aside work that still needs to be worked on. I also set up the TOC information for myself, or in the event something happens to me overnight – for someone else. I signed out for the day, handed in my keys and that was that.

I look forward to my next couple of days in this classroom. I am glad I know where items are, and that I have a prep block to write some notes for the regular classroom teacher on the time I have spent in her classroom.

### May 11, 2018

Wow I was so lucky to get this placement for my first TOC teaching opportunity! Her TOC planning was impeccable! Each day was organized via folders, each day Plan was written up precisely, and the students made it super easy to slip into their teacher's place. I was able to find everything so easily (student computer passwords, check!), and the staff was great!

### May 14, 2018

My first day as a TOC in Merritt SD58. I got to teach a grade 1/2 class, and once again the teacher left great detailed notes, and actually showed up in the morning to give me a bit of an orientation to her school and classroom! Her students were just lovely to work with. I also had support workers in my room, to assist with a couple of students, who helped me out as well. Today I realized that support workers are integral to keeping a school community (and classroom community) running smoothly.

### May 15, 2018

My first day teaching in a French immersion school! Luckily it was a Kindergarten, grade 1 class. These young students ran a tight ship! They were very knowledgeable and helped me out with my French pronunciation. I found I remembered more than I thought I would.

### May 17, 2018

My first day at two different TOC assignments.
   Morning: grade 3 classroom
   Afternoon: Grade 10, 11, and 12 Art class
   It was interesting to switch from primary mode, to secondary mode. I felt like I was "on" in the morning with the grade 3's. They need so much direction, and were great to work with. However, the secondary students were very laid back and I felt more like "just an adult in the room." The secondary students had their various assignments, and the only time they interacted with me was when I asked them about their work (which I did because it was fascinating!) or if they needed to use the restroom. Frankly, I was surprised they even remembered to ask me to use the restroom.
   This day gave me the experience of Elementary vs. Secondary. Although, I do believe the middling years between the two sets of grades would be more of a deciding factor to my own personal sense of preference.

### May 22, 2018

Today is all about being a prep teacher, and a French as a Second Language prep teacher to boot! Fortunately, the FSL teacher left behind a great assignment for the students to complete (Directions to add pieces to the drawing of a house: i.e., dessine un la porte). Each class was very different, but I do believe all students were relieved to see (and hear) a non-French speaking teacher teaching them French. Perhaps they believed I would be more sympathetic to their second language learning plight (I was, to a certain extent). So, I taught French as a Second Language for grades 4–6, and each of them did this exercise. The grade 6's were able to go onto the next activity: Dessine animaux – draw an animal; criteria, it must have at least two different types of animals merged into the one drawing (i.e., la lapinhibou – I tell you, the drawing example for this assignment was quite frightening)! I taught Fine Arts to the final class of the day, a grade 4/5 class. Boy were these students ready for the end of the day! They seem to be a high energy class to begin with but having the great news that their teacher's wife just had a new baby, having a substitute (TOC) for the day, then having me come in to teach them their Fine Arts was a bit much for them. Their excitement couldn't be contained. We ended up wrapping up a previous art project (fish landscape with mod podged tissue for underwater plants), then doing a class-wide clean-up. The day flew by, it was so much fun! I must admit I was intimidated by the thought of teaching FSL today, but it was much easier than anticipated. I have no more qualms now about teaching FSL. In fact, I am finding that TOCing is getting a lot easier as I go and teach.

### May 23, 2018

Today was another unexpected experience. I taught basic Secwepemctsin greetings and introductions to the TRU faculty and staff this morning. Really? It isn't much different! They still need to be kept on track, and they were still interested in their learning. It made it much easier to teach them so well.

### May 24, 2018

I taught my first intermediate class today. A grade 5/6 class. I was a bit apprehensive about working with them, but they were great. They tried to flex their boundaries a bit, and I let them know that my boundaries did not go that much further than their own classroom teacher. Although I heard she keeps a tight rein on them, so maybe I was a bit of a break for them today. At any rate, they were a great class to work with. I really liked seeing the young entrepreneur booklet they were working out of, and their social studies government project menu (they choose projects that add up to at least 50 points) was a super good idea! Working as a TOC I get to see so much more than I would have if I had gotten a full-time teaching job right away. And I have to admit that I took pictures of this teacher's classroom set up! I think this is one of the things I am most worried about when I get my own classroom. What will it look like? Will I manage to keep it not too cluttered? Will it be inviting to my students? Will it reflect what we are learning? These are just some of the questions I ask myself as I see other teachers' classrooms.

### May 25, 2018

Morning: Another TRU basic Secwépemc Greetings & Introductions lesson. Adults can be just as nervous about what they are learning about as youngsters. I had been so nervous about teaching adults, but they make it fun! We have come up with what some of the sounds of Secwepemctsin sound like. For example, "c" sounds like the end of a record playing "ccccc." I know that I would never teach younger students in some ways that I am teaching them, but I have had to use my newfound elementary teaching skills on my adult class!

Afternoon: Another intermediate class, this time out in Rayleigh. It was an easy afternoon. Gym, clean-up and free time. The teacher left great instructions for me for the afternoon, so I knew who to use for help within the class. The most interesting interactions happen at this age group. You see the petty arguing of some of the boys and girls and WE know that they are beginning to see each other in a different light and therefore are more likely to pick on each other to get their attention, but THEY do not see that that is what they are doing. Puberty is definitely a complicated event in young students' lives!

### May 28, 2018

Morning: My third of four TRU basic Secwepemctsin greetings and introductions class. We had a great discussion about whether they should invite a student in the class to give the acknowledgement of the Indigenous territory (ONLY if they absolutely know they are from that territory). We determined that this puts too much pressure on the student, and instead agreed that they could begin the acknowledgements, and first question the entire class if anyone, who is from the territory, would like to step up to formally acknowledge the territory. If not, then they as the instructor/TRU staff members will proceed, respectfully. It is funny because these are some of the things that I struggle with as an Indigenous person myself. I grew up on reserve, however my community lost much of our traditions. An example, I have had contradictory advice about standing/sitting during drumming. I was told that only honour songs should everyone stand for. Well nowadays everyone stands for any old drum song being sung. And I know for a fact that not all songs are honour songs. This is something that I have to confirm with my Elders. Usually, I will follow the direction of the eldest Elder in the room. If they stand, or indicate that you should stand, I stand. If not, then I usually remain sitting. Half the time I know that many participants do not want to be disrespectful, so they stand up to all drum songs. To me it feels as if we are standing midway through a symphony, just because they started playing their music. It feels odd. So, I will consult with the Elders on this issue.

### May 29, 2018

My first requested TOC position, a return to the grade 3 classroom at Kay Bingham.

Another great day! I got to incorporate my Indigenous teachings into the set lessons for the day. I was left the book Nanabosho Dances by Joe McLellan, and in it the story mentions sweet grass and tobacco, as well as powwow dancing. For our body break I had the students dance to "Powwow Sweat – Men's Fancy; Women's Traditional." As well I brought in, from my car, a braid of sweet grass and some sage. I let the students know that traditional "tobacco" is much different than what they know as cigarette tobacco. And then I let them know that our tobacco was used to offer up to the animals when hunting (as told in the story) but also when gathering plants and berries. I then brought the sweet grass and sage around for the students to smell and experience. It was a beautifully inserted mini lesson.

### May 30, 2018

My final TRU Secwépemc Basic Greetings and Introductions class.

This class went well. Teaching adults wasn't nearly as scary as I thought it would be. Everyone was understanding and knowing that they were feeling out of depth with their pronunciation, and that was what they wanted out of the class, made these classes easy to teach.

### May 31, 2018

Merritt Central Elementary – grade 2/3 class.

Play is the way. This is such a great program! I watched the students go through a game this morning that was all about leading and following. Letting the leaders lead, and the followers trust their leader. I want to look into this program to learn more.

### June 1, 2018

Cultural Day at Kay Bingham Elementary – my first requested TOC position! Storytelling all day.

Today was all about storytelling. I told my favourite Secwépemc stories, and a couple of string stories that I adapted from a booklet I found online "String Stories." Today schools from across North Kamloops, and a few classes from Barrier, came to enjoy Aboriginal culture. There were games, crafts, stories, food! It was a great day to participate in.

### June 4, 2018

Collettville Elementary in Merritt, BC – French Immersion School… EEK!

Today I was a floating teacher as I was the TOC for the school Learning Resource Teacher. I stepped into the primary classrooms to mind the students as their teacher did reading assessments, and Kindergarten assessments. Luckily the students were all very good dealing with a non-French speaking TOC.

### June 6, 2018

Rayleigh Elementary – grade 3.

Today was great! This grade 3 class was helpful with their routines. I even learned how to draw a butterfly on a flower along with the students. A great online directed drawing website: https://www.artforkidshub.com/how-to-draw-a-butterfly-on-a-flower/. I will definitely be taking this resource along with me!!!!

### June 11, 2018

Logan Lake Secondary – Social Studies.

I got to go into another secondary school and "teach" a social studies class. Well, I got to supervise a social studies class in the library while they continued work that they already had. I only had one block of social studies, at the very end of the day. They were working on their echo projects. Here is an online example of what students can do via echo projects: https://www.thielmann.ca/echo-project-examples.html.

Today I also found out that I was accepted into the TRU Master of Education program! I will begin my graduate studies this September 2018.

### June 12, 2018

Marion Schilling Elementary – Grade 3 morning only.

Wow it was great to be back into a school I am so familiar with! To greet the staff and know the students in the hallways. This TOC job made me realize the value of having a continuing position in a school. You get to know your school community. Be part of a school community. The grade 3's I worked with today only knew me from Kindergarten (that was the grade they were in when I last worked at this school), and a few remembered me. It was funny to see the looks on the faces of the students who thought they could pull the wool over my eyes because they couldn't remember ME! Ha! It was a great morning, but I realized that the end of year excitement was starting already in this class. It was a bit hard to get work done this morning as all the students just wanted to be outside ("can we go outside, Miss Marie, and do our work?"). It is interesting to see the end of year excitement begin. You start to notice it is harder and harder to get students to do any sort of work.

### June 13, 2018

Westsyde Secondary – full day.

    Well, I made arrangements with the teacher about today. I let him know that I would be bringing my mother along as a guest speaker for the full day. Art is not my best subject, and definitely not secondary art! And forget about photography! SO, thankfully, I know that my mother, being a photographer herself and a crafty person, would love to share her knowledge! Thank goodness!!!!!! We had a blast working with students ranging from grade 8–12. I noticed as the age/grade of the student rose, so too did their respect level rise. Not that the grade 8 and 9's were severely disrespectful, it was just a general level of not wanting to be in the classroom at all. I think what made that particular class a bit more chaotic was that we had a grade-level assembly throughout that block. So, whenever we got into our discussions, a different grade would get called out and this disrupted out class. This just further made me realize that you have to be flexible as a teacher. I also found out that on Wednesdays, as a connections block at the end of the day, a TOC must hang out in the library to help out those students who need help. I floundered a bit about this part of the day. Luckily one of the secretaries helped me figure out where I was supposed to be.

### June 14, 2018

Haldane Elementary – grade 5.

    WOW! What an organized classroom! I really enjoy TOCing at classrooms in which I can just slip in and follow the list of assigned work. The students were awesome too! I suppose it helped that I had a prep block first thing, so I was able to familiarize myself with the entire classroom before I actually had to teach. Math problem-solving as an anchor activity for math. I like it!

## June 15, 2018

Kay Bingham Elementary – grade 5/6.

Requested again! YES! I love working with a classroom I already know! Today we had Eureka Science come into our classroom and teach all about climate change. The activities they did were right in the students' ZPD! I think I'll "borrow" their activity ideas for my own science projects!

## June 18, 2018

Haldane Elementary – grade 5.

Requested again!!!! I absolutely love teaching this class. What a lovely bunch of students. This class made me realize that TOCing is mostly easy. You get to work with lovely students, most of the time. I remember prior to starting my TOC position that I was worried about going into classrooms and not being able to control the students. I'm glad that I learned classroom management skills in my teaching program! Classroom management really is 98% of teaching!

## June 19, 2018

Barrier Secondary.

Passion projects! That is what I took away from today's secondary TOCing experience! This week all of the students are working on their passion projects. Here are some of the projects I witnessed:

- Students out fishing (heard students calling into the secretary first thing this morning)
- A student was working on whether she could turn fake fog a different colour
- Quite a few students decided to create their own video games (and isn't that a great way of getting to play video games all day long at school?!)
- 4 young grade 9 boys created their ideal basketball teams using statistics (overall career points)
- 1 grade 11 young man was determining if free throws were done better one way or another (repetitive motion, or something like that)
- A grade 12 young woman was making her own grape jelly and bread to make a peanut butter and jelly sandwich
- A grade 10 young woman was creating an information board about traditional Aboriginal plants
- All range of grades were working on soapbox carts for a race happening on Friday

- A grade 10 girl was creating her own kayak from scratch!
- As you can tell, this was a wonderful day of TOCing! I just wish I could get called in on Friday for their presentations!

### June 20, 2018

Diamondvale Elementary – grade 4.

PE TOCing is great! My first two classes were all about PE. We played tags games mostly, student choice (they all chose zombie tag... in the dark!).

The remainder of the morning and afternoon was teaching a grade 4/5 classroom. Wrapping up math projects, and an afternoon of watching a movie (Polar Express). Today was further evidence that students are definitely ready for summer!!!!!

### June 22, 2018

Kamloops School of the Arts – Social Studies.

Well, I got a TOC position for the afternoon today "teaching" Social Studies. I got to the school and found out that instead it was going to be all about a students vs. teachers softball game. So, I took attendance (found out that the majority of my class went straight to the game), then went outside for the softball game. It went for the majority of the afternoon; teachers will be able to brag about winning for another year. Then there was about 1/2 hour left in the day. I went back to the classroom, as I had a prep block I got to sit and read one of the teacher's classroom novels. It wasn't until this part of the day that I realized that today was the very last day of school for the secondary students! A lot of things clicked into place once I remembered... empty hallways, only 7 students checking in for attendance, softball game... just all last day type of activities.

### June 25, 2018

Merritt Central Elementary – grade 2/3.

Today I took away the big/little buddy end of year party. We got to go outside with the buddies to hang out and play together. There was the ever-present playground, basketball, skipping, and stuffies. We topped all that off with a snack of cookies and cupcakes. I was VERY glad that we did this snack just before lunch. This school also does their lunches differently than I have seen in other schools. Their students have lunch in the lunchroom. Then they go out to play. I have only worked in schools where the students ate at their desks, so this was interesting to see. A great way of supervising students all in one place, instead of having to step into different classrooms throughout lunch.

## June 26, 2018

Marion Schilling Elementary – cultural day.

Again, I was able to return to the school I worked in as an Aboriginal Education Worker. I loved being able to see all of the students throughout the school! Wow have they grown!!!!

I helped out in the Kindergarten class for the whole morning. We had another TOC in for the regular classroom teacher, and she did not know how to do the craft activity (turtle shakers! A great craft!). This was fun, hanging out with the youngest bunch of students was a great way to start the morning. The assembly was a surprise! I was gifted with a drum from the school! And to top off this, I had to SING with my new drum! Thank goodness we sang the Secwépemc Welcome Song since I already know this song.

The afternoon I was in the library doing the storytelling workshop. I got to do string stories and tell my favourite two Secwepemc stories: Coyote Juggles His eyes; and, How Bear Lost His Tail.

It was a wonderful event, where schools from the South side of Kamloops got to come and experience Aboriginal culture for the day.

## Overall Reflections of May and June 2018

This last two months of Teaching On Call (TOC) experience has been eye opening… in a great way! I am more confident as a teacher, and I know that I can work with a classroom full of students on a whim. I have seen many different types of classrooms, and many types of assignments and projects that I want to do when I get into a regular classroom. The one thing I worry about are the effects of knowing that I taught students at the end of the year. Students who were more worried about when they could go outside, or when summer vacation was going to start. I wonder how it will be working with students during the regular school year? I hope it is just as great as I have known it these past two months. And now I know that TOCing is not the hardship that I worried about before officially starting my teaching career.

Now I know that I will be returning to my own studies in the Fall, I hope to continue Teaching On Call in Kamloops. I believe that it will be too hard to continue as a TOC in both Kamloops and Merritt, so I may have to give up my Merritt position. I have enjoyed working in the Merritt School District. I will keep this school district in mind for the future.

My next steps will be to assess whether I can manage both graduate studies and Teaching On Call. I knew that trying to get a full, or even a part-time, teaching position would be too hard to do on top of my graduate studies. I have even been advised that working and studying may not work for me. I do not want to spread myself too thin. I Have taken the graduate program advisors' advice and just stayed on the TOC list for the fall and not tried out for a term-certain or continuing teaching position.

YAY! Summer! And... oh no! Summer! I get to enjoy my summer break, but I also get to worry about my summer break... and my break from a pay cheque! Luckily, I have a small summer job, but this is also something that I am keeping in mind for future teaching positions. I hope that there will be a system whereby I can funnel some of my regular pay into summer pay cheques. Otherwise, I will have to be very conscientious of my savings throughout the year (EEK! I must admit this is not my strong suit at all!!!). Well, I guess that is on my list of wait and see.

## September 10, 2018

Barriere Elementary – grade 4/5 class.

Wow what a great class to get back into the swing of things as a TOC for the new school year! Today I had a wonderful time working with the students and learning about a new type of "maker project." It was called "The Most Magnificent Thing." The students had to create something from a cardboard box and keep track of it and see how their plans for their Thing changed as they created. I really appreciated seeing this new project!

Today I also worked with a student in the class with an exceptionality. We had to adjust the PE class to accommodate her, but she was gung-ho about participating in the entire team relay that I had planned out for them. I spoke to her afterwards and her reflection was that perhaps some of the relay was not really for her, but that I had given them all options to make team adjustments for each team member.

## September 24, 2018

Parkview Elementary – grade 5/6 class.

I felt off balance all day today. This was an assignment that was clearly organized early this morning. The day plan was great, and effective... but "I" was not ready or in the frame of mind to teach this morning. I was lucky to receive a great group of students who were very receptive to my teaching. They were very accepting of my Indigenous perspective, and a bit curious too. I guess it helped that today I was asked to teach a bit about "Orange Shirt Day" and Residential Schools. They had a teacher they could ask those personal questions to. I was not surprised to see that a couple of the students in the class were emotionally affected after hearing about the story. I handled them softly and made sure they knew I was available to talk to. They did end up opening up to me about what the assignment made them think about, and it broke my heart to hear their stories. I believe they felt better by days end, but I made a note to their regular classroom teacher to check in with them again the next day (or whenever they would return).

The classroom was unique. Their teacher, over the summer, built a class "fortress" for them to use for reading or doing their work. It has an inside area, and an upper balcony. I got the feeling from the kids that they appreciate their teacher, and how much he values them as his students. It was a great atmosphere to spend the day teaching within.

# References

Avsec, S., & Kocijancic, S. (2016). A path model of effective technology-intensive inquiry-based learning. *Educational Technology & Society, 19*(1), 308–320.

Battiste, M. (2002). *Indigenous knowledge and pedagogy in First Nations education: A literature review with recommendations*. Apamuwek Institute.

British Columbia Ministry of Education. (2021). https://curriculum.gov.bc.ca/competencies

Bullock, S. M., & Peercy, M. M. (2018). Crossing boundaries to challenge the self-study methodology: Affordances and critiques. In D. G. A. Ovens (Ed.), *Pushing boundaries and crossing borders: Self-study as a means for researching pedagogy* (pp. 19–25). S-STEP.

Bullough, R. V. (2014). Recalling 40 years of teacher education in the USA: A personal essay. *Journal of Education for Teaching, 40*(5), 474–491. https://doi.org/10.1080/02607476.2014.956537

Burney, S. (2012). *Pedagogy of the other: Edward Said, postcolonial theory and strategies for critique*. Peter Lang Publishing, Inc.

Chan, E. Y., & Ng, S. S. (2012). Narrative inquiry as pedagogy in a blended learning environment. *International Journal of Learning, 18*(11), 145–154.

Ciuffetelli Parker, D. (2011). Related literacy narratives: Letters as a narrative inquiry method in teacher education. In J. Kitchen, D. Ciuffetelli Parker, & D. Pushor (Eds.), *Narrative inquiries into curriculum making in teacher education* (Advances in Research on Teaching, Vol. 13, pp. 131–149). Emerald Group Publishing Limited.

Clandinin, D. J. (1986). *Classroom practice: Teacher images in action*. Farmer Press.

Clandinin, D. J. (Ed.). (2007). *Handbook of narrative inquiry: Mapping a methodology*. Sage Publications.

Clandinin, D. J., & Connelly, F. M. (2000). *Narrative inquiry: Experience and story in qualitative research*. Jossey-Bass.

Connelly, F. M., & Clandinin, D. J. (1988). *Teachers as curriculum planners: Narratives of experience*. Teachers College, Columbia University.

Coulter, C., Michael, C., & Poynor, L. (2007). Storytelling as pedagogy: An unexpected outcome of narrative inquiry. *Curriculum Inquiry, 37*(2), 103–122.

Craig, C. J. (2008). Joseph Schwab, self-study of teaching and teacher education practices proponent: A personal perspective. *Teaching and Teacher Education, 24*(8), 1993–2001.

Craig, C. J. (2011). Narrative inquiry in teaching and teacher education. In J. Kitchen, D. Ciuffetelli Parker, & D. Pushor (Eds.), *Narrative inquiries into curriculum making in teacher education* (Advances in Research on Teaching, Vol. 13) (pp. 19–42). Emerald Group Publishing Limited.

# REFERENCES

Dewey, J. (1938). *Experience and education*. Collier books.
Edmunds, A., Nickel, J., & Badley, K. (2015). *Educational foundations in Canada*. Oxford University Press.
Egbo, B. (2009). *Teaching for diversity in Canadian schools*. Pearson Canada.
Elbaz-Luwisch, F. (2010). Writing and professional learning: The uses of autobiography in graduate studies in education. *Teachers and Teaching: Theory and Practice, 16*(3), 307–327.
Ellis, C. S., & Bochner, A. (2000). Autoethnography, personal narrative, reflexivity: Researcher as subject. In N. Denzin & Y. Lincoln (Eds.), *The handbook of qualitative research* (pp. 733–768). Sage.
Etherington, K. (2006). Reflexivity: Using our 'selves' in narrative research. In S. Trahar (Ed.), *Narrative Research on learning: Comparative and international perspectives* (pp. 77–92). Symposium Books.
Farrell, J. P. (1986). *The national unified school in Allende's Chile. The role of education in the destruction of a revolution*. University of British Columbia Press.
Geertz, C. (1995). *After the fact: Two countries, four decades, one anthropologist*. Harvard University Press.
Ghosh, R., & Abdi, A. A. (2013). *Education and the politics of difference* (2nd ed.). Canadian Scholars' Press.
Gilroy, P. (2014). International teacher education: Changing times, changing practices. *Journal of Education for Teaching, 40*(5), 445–446. https://doi.org/10.1080/02607476.2014.957995
Gnidec, A. (2008). *Teaching for diversity and social justice throughout the K-12 curriculum*. http://www.bced.gov.bc.ca/irp/pdfs/making_space/mkg_spc_intr.pdf
Hawley, W. D. (1990). The education of Japanese teachers: Lessons for the United States. In E. B. Gumbert (Ed.), *Fit to teach: Teacher education in international perspective* (pp. 31–62). Center for Cross-Cultural Education, Georgia State University.
Hayhoe, R. (2000). Redeeming modernity. *Comparative Education Review, 44*(2), 423–488.
Howe, E. R. (2000). *Secondary school teachers' conceptions of critical thinking in British Columbia and Japan: A comparative study* [MA thesis, University of British Columbia]. ERIC Document Reproduction Service No. ED 451099.
Howe, E. R. (2005a). *Japan's teacher acculturation: A comparative ethongraphic narrative of teacher induction* [Unpublished doctoral dissertation]. University of Toronto.
Howe, E. R. (2005b). Japan's teacher acculturation: Critical analysis through comparative ethnographic narrative. *Journal of Education for Teaching, 31*(2), 121–131. https://doi.org/10.1080/02607470500127251
Howe, E. R. (2009). Internationalization of higher education in East Asia: A comparative ethnographic narrative of Japanese universities. *Research in Comparative and International Education, 4*(4), 384–392. http://www.wwwords.co.uk/RCIE/content/pdfs/4/issue4_4.asp

Howe, E. R. (2010). A comparative ethnographic narrative approach to studying teacher acculturation. In V. L. Masemman & S. Majhanovich (Eds.), *Papers in memory of David N. Wilson: Clamouring for a better world* (pp. 121–136). Sense Publishers.

Howe, E. R. (2017). Experience, education and story: A transcultural teacher narrative. In M. Etherington (Ed.), *What teachers need to know: Topics of inclusion* (pp. 272–285). Wipf and Stock.

Howe, E. R. (2018a, November 6). *Music also matters in the real world.* The Conversation. http://theconversation.com/music-also-matters-in-the-real-world-104388

Howe, E. R. (2018b, September 5). Let's teach students why math matters in the real world. *The Conversation.* http://theconversation.com/lets-teach-students-why-math-matters-in-the-real-world-102316

Howe, E. R., & Arimoto, M. (2014). Narrative teacher education pedagogies from across the Pacific. In C. Craig & L. Orland-Barak (Eds.), *International teacher education: Promising pedagogies advances in research on teaching* (Part A) (Vol. 22, pp. 217–236). Emerald.

Howe, E. R., & Cope Watson, G. (2020). S-STEP in comparative and international education: Comparative ethnographic narrative. In C. Edge, A. Cameron-Standerford, & B. Bergh (Eds.), *Textiles and tapestries.* EdTech Books. https://edtechbooks.org/textiles_tapestries_self_study/chapter_116

Howe, E. R., & Xu, S. (2013). Transcultural teacher development within the dialectic of the global and local: Bridging gaps between East and West. *Teaching and Teacher Education, 36*, 33–43.

Huber, J., Caine, V., Huber, M., & Steeves, P. (2013). Narrative inquiry as pedagogy in education: The extraordinary potential of living, telling, retelling, and reliving stories of experience. *Review of Research in Education, 37*(1), 212–242.

Iftody, T. (2013). Letting experience in at the front door and bringing theory through the back: Exploring the pedagogical possibilities of situated self-narration in teacher education. *Teachers and Teaching: Theory and Practice, 19*(4), 382–397.

Kitchen, J. (2009). Passages: Improving teacher education through narrative self-study. In D. Tidwell, M. Heston, & L. Fitzgerald (Eds.), *Research methods for the self-study of practice* (pp. 35–51). Springer.

Kosnik, C., & Beck, C. (2010). *Redesigning a teacher education program: A story of our challenges and successes* [Paper presentation]. The 8th international conference on self-study of teacher education practices. Navigating the public and private: Negotiating the diverse landscape of teacher education, East Sussex, England.

LaBoskey, V. K. (2004). The methodology of self-study and its theoretical underpinnings. In J. J. Loughran, M. L. Hamilton, V. K. LaBoskey, & T. Russell (Eds.), *International handbook of self-study of teaching and teacher education practices* (pp. 817–869). Springer.

Latta, M. M., & Kim, J. H. (2011). Investing in the curricular lives of educators: Narrative inquiry as pedagogical medium. *Journal of Curriculum Studies, 43*(5), 679–695.

LeTendre, G. K. (1999). The problem of Japan: Qualitative studies and international educational comparisons. *Educational Researcher, 28*(2), 38–46.

LeTendre, G. K. (2000). *Learning to be adolescent: Growing up in U.S. and Japanese middle schools.* Yale University Press.

Lillard, A. S. (2005). *Montessori: The science behind the genius.* Oxford University Press.

Loughran, J. (2007). Researching teacher education practices: Responding to the challenges, demands, and expectations of self-study. *Journal of Teacher Education, 58*(1), 12–20. https://doi.org/10.1177/0022487106296217

Loughran, J. (2010). Seeking knowledge for teaching teaching: Moving beyond stories. *Studying Teacher Education, 6*(3), 221–226.

Loughran, J., Hamilton, M. L., LaBoskey, V. K., & Russell, T. (Eds.). (2004). *International handbook of self-study of teaching and teacher education practices.* Springer.

Masemann, V. L. (1982). Critical ethnography in the study of comparative education. *Comparative Education Review, 26*(1), 1–15.

Mulcahy, D. G. (2010). Redefining without undermining liberal education. *Innovative Higher Education, 35*(3), 203–214. https://doi.org/10.1007/s10755-010-9137-9

Nakane, C. (1970). *Japanese society.* University of California Press.

Ni, P. S. (2014). *12 empowering and uplifting quotes on diversity & inclusion.* https://www.psychologytoday.com/blog/communication-success/201401/12-empowering-and-uplifting-quotes-diversity-inclusion

Nussbaum, M. (2004). Liberal education and global community. *Liberal Education, 90*(1), 42–47. http://files.eric.ed.gov/fulltext/EJ728534.pdf

Okano, K. (1993). *School to work transition in Japan: An ethnographic study.* Multilingual Matters Ltd.

Perkins, D. (1992). *Smart schools: From training memories to educating minds.* The Free Press.

Pewewardy, C. (2002). Learning styles of American Indian/Alaska native students: A review of the literature and implications for practice. *Journal of American Indian Education, 41*(3). https://www.tru.ca/__shared/assets/Pewewardy_2002_Learning_styles_Aboriginal23616.pdf

Pinnegar, S., & Daynes, J. G. (2007). Locating narrative inquiry historically: Thematics in the turn to narrative. In D. J. Clandinin (Ed.), *Handbook of narrative inquiry.* Sage Publications.

Rodriguez, T. L. (2011). Stories of self, stories of practice: Enacting a vision of socially just pedagogy for Latino youth. *Teaching Education, 22*(3), 239–254.

Rohlen, T. P. (1983). *Japan's high schools.* University of California Press.

Rohlen, T. P., & LeTendre, G. K. (Eds.). (1996). *Teaching and learning in Japan*. Cambridge University Press.

Sato, N. (1991). *Ethnography of Japanese elementary schools: Quest for equality* [Unpublished doctoral dissertation]. Stanford University.

Schwab, J. J. (1983). The practical 4: Something for curriculum professors to do. *Curriculum Inquiry, 13*(3), 239–265.

Sewell, A. (2002). Constructivism and student misconceptions: Why every teacher needs to know about them. *Australian Science Teachers' Journal, 48*(4), 24–28. http://eds.a.ebscohost.com.ezproxy.tru.ca/eds/pdfviewer/pdfviewer?sid= 8ea555d0-9d01-41c8-a860-420fdf42d851%40sessionmgr103&vid=25&hid=4111

Shimahara, N. K., & Sakai, A. (1995). *Learning to teach in two cultures: Japan and the United States*. Garland Publishing, Inc.

Sinclair, N., & Dainard, S. (2020). Sixties scoop. In *The Canadian encyclopedia*. https://www.thecanadianencyclopedia.ca/en/article/sixties-scoop

Spradley, J. P. (1979). *The ethnographic interview*. Holt, Rinehart & Winston.

Stelt, T. N. V. (1995). *Cooperative learning: Does it work and do students like it?* http://scholarworks.gvsu.edu/cgi/viewcontent.cgi?article=1224&context=theses

Stevenson, H., & Stigler, J. (1992). *The learning gap: Why our schools are failing and what we can learn from Japanese and Chinese education*. Summit Books.

Stribling, S. M., DeMulder, E. K., Barnstead, S., & Dallman, L. (2015). The teaching philosophy: An opportunity to guide practice or an exercise in futility? *Teacher Educators' Journal, 2015*, 37–50.

Takakura, S., & Murata, Y. (Eds.). (1998). *Education in Japan – A bilingual text: Present system and tasks/curriculum and instruction*. Gakken.

Trahar, S. (2011). Changing landscapes, shifting identities in higher education: Narratives of academics in the UK. *Research in Education, 86*, 46–60.

Truth and Reconciliation Commission of Canada. (2015). *Calls to action*. http://www.trc.ca/websites/trcinstitution/File/2015/Findings/Calls_to_Action_English2.Pdf

Veenman, M., Hout-Wolters, B., & Afflerbach, P. (2006). Metacognition and learning: Conceptual and methodological considerations. *Metacognition & Learning, 1*(1), 3. https://doi.org/10.1007/s11409-006-6893-0

Weissner, S., & Battiste, M. (n.d.). The 2000 revision of the United Nations draft principles and guidelines on the protection of the heritage of Indigenous people. *St. Thomas Law Review, 13*(1), 383–414.

Xu, S. J. (2011). Narrative inquiry in curriculum of life on expanded and extended landscapes in transition. In D. C. Parker, D. Pushor, & J. Kitchen (Eds.), *On narrative inquiries into curriculum-making in teacher education* (pp. 263–280). Emerald.

Xu, S. J., & Connelly, F. M. (2009). Narrative inquiry for teacher education and development: Focus on English as a foreign language in China. *Teaching and Teacher Education, 25*(2), 219–227.

Yonemura, M. (1982). Teacher conversations: A potential source for their own professional growth. *Curriculum Inquiry, 12*(3), 239–256.

Zeichner, K. (2014). The struggle for the soul of teaching and teacher education in the USA. *Journal of Education for Teaching, 40*(5), 551–568. https://doi.org/10.1080/02607476.2014.956544

# Index

administrator   13, 14, 27, 44, 46, 63, 64, 66, 75, 80, 82, 83, 95, 127, 135, 143
assessment   XVI, 10, 35, 45, 51, 52, 60–62, 75, 153

class   XI, 2, 5–10, 12, 22–24, 26, 29, 33–36, 38, 40, 42–44, 47, 49, 53–58, 61, 63–65, 67, 70–72, 74–76, 78, 81, 82, 85, 87, 89, 93, 96, 99–101, 104, 111, 112, 117–119, 122–129, 131, 133, 135, 136, 138–140, 148–159
comparative ethnographic narrative   1, 4, 12–17
COVID-19   XVI, XVII, 18, 46, 118, 119, 124, 125, 128, 131, 135, 136, 143
critical thinking   78, 120, 121, 123, 132, 133
culture   XVII, 2, 50, 56, 72, 76, 94, 97, 98, 100, 104, 111, 122, 153, 157
curriculum   XVI, 4, 7, 12, 15, 16, 24, 34, 43, 47, 49–52, 54, 56, 59–62, 68, 74–78, 83, 99–101, 107, 114, 120, 122, 126, 136, 140, 141

diversity   XI, XVI, 41, 92, 122, 125, 138, 143

elementary   4, 7, 8, 21, 28, 29, 31–33, 42, 43, 49, 52, 58, 59, 66, 68, 77, 81, 84, 90, 95, 98, 110, 112, 114, 116, 124, 126, 128, 131, 134, 135, 137, 138, 140, 149, 151–158
English   5, 7–9, 11, 16, 23, 28, 29, 31, 39, 49, 51, 53, 57, 71, 72, 74, 75, 78, 80, 85, 90–93, 99–102, 104, 105, 107, 116, 118, 126, 137, 146
equity   XVI, 24, 101, 129, 133, 143
ethnicity   XVII, 2, 22, 23
evaluation   10, 35, 61, 62, 65, 67

gender   XVII, 2, 26, 80, 82, 90, 100, 101, 119, 122, 129, 140, 143

history   2, 51, 57, 68, 73, 78, 84, 106, 111, 146
home economics   19, 20, 33, 34, 36, 37, 39, 40, 143

inclusion   XI, XVI, 129, 133, 137, 138, 141, 143

Indigenous   XI, XVII, 2, 41, 51, 104–108, 111, 113, 114, 125, 126, 140, 141, 143
induction   12, 14, 27, 74, 75, 78, 92, 94

K-12   36, 86, 140

leadership   XI, 32, 46, 50, 64–66, 78, 81, 82, 121, 134, 141
Lesbian, Gay, Bisexual, Transgender, Queer (LGBTQ)   83, 137–139, 141, 143, 146, 147
literacy   16, 70–72, 100, 110, 120, 132, 134, 136

math   28, 33, 34, 47, 50, 51, 53, 55, 64, 78, 99–101, 154, 156
music   29, 54, 63–67, 73, 78, 90–92, 143, 152

narrative inquiry   XI, 1, 2, 12–16, 77, 78

philosophy   XI, 2, 7, 10, 14, 17, 28, 29, 54, 59, 66, 68, 70, 71, 73, 77–79, 84, 91, 101, 113, 114, 116, 120, 122, 123, 129, 131–133
physical education   42, 51, 58, 80, 81, 98, 126
professional development   14, 30, 49, 65, 75, 78, 86, 114, 138, 141

race   XVII, 2, 22, 41, 98, 99, 133, 155
relationships   5, 18, 27–29, 32, 55, 65, 81, 93, 94, 96, 105, 107–109, 138
religion   XVII, 2, 43, 44, 64
rural   XII, 28–30, 41, 53, 65, 68–71, 81, 83, 90, 116, 118, 119, 143, 145, 147

science   4–6, 12, 33, 37, 39, 42, 43, 53, 73–75, 78, 81, 84, 114, 155
secondary   XI, 1, 24, 33, 35, 36, 41–43, 49, 51, 53, 58, 59, 63, 68, 73, 81, 137, 138, 145, 149, 153–156
self-study   1, 2, 13, 16
Sexual Orientation and Gender Identity (SOGI)   80–83, 140, 141
sexuality   XVII, 2, 82, 146
socials   6, 27, 32, 35, 43, 58, 59, 64, 69, 73, 78, 81, 83, 84, 87, 89, 94, 99, 102, 107, 113, 116, 120, 121, 132, 133, 137, 138, 140, 141, 143

socioeconomic status   2, 46, 65, 80, 125
special education   35, 47, 51, 52, 54, 59, 84, 86, 138, 143

teacher conversations   1, 12, 13, 17, 18, 27, 28, 46, 72, 76, 77, 85, 101
Teacher Teaching on Call (TTOC)   81, 86, 112, 118, 125, 138

technology   XVI, 16, 17, 52, 61, 62, 122, 123, 130, 136

university   XI, XII, 7, 8, 12, 18, 20, 28, 33, 41, 42, 45, 51–53, 59, 60, 63, 64, 68, 72, 73, 76, 78, 80, 84, 91–94, 99, 100, 107, 110, 111, 116, 124, 131, 137, 138, 140, 145
urban   XII, 30, 41, 64, 68, 83, 143, 145

Printed in the United States
by Baker & Taylor Publisher Services